Tai Chi

Unlocking the Power of an Internal Chinese Martial Art,

Including the 24 Forms and Meditation Techniques for Beginners

© Copyright 2021

The contents of this book may not be reproduced, duplicated or transmitted without direct written permission from the author.

Under no circumstances will any legal responsibility or blame be held against the publisher for any reparation, damages, or monetary loss due to the information herein, either directly or indirectly.

Legal Notice:

This book is copyright protected. This is only for personal use. You cannot amend, distribute, sell, use, quote or paraphrase any part or the content within this book without the consent of the author.

Disclaimer Notice:

Please note the information contained within this document is for educational and entertainment purposes only. Every attempt has been made to provide accurate, up to date and reliable complete information. No warranties of any kind are expressed or implied. Readers acknowledge that the author is not engaging in the rendering of legal, financial, medical or professional advice. The content of this book has been derived from various sources. Please consult a licensed professional before attempting any techniques outlined in this book.

By reading this document, the reader agrees that under no circumstances is the author responsible for any losses, direct or indirect, which are incurred as a result of the use of information contained within this document, including, but not limited to, —errors, omissions, or inaccuracies.

Your Free Gift (only available for a limited time)

Thanks for getting this book! If you want to learn more about various spirituality topics, then join Mari Silva's community and get a free guided meditation MP3 for awakening your third eye. This guided meditation mp3 is designed to open and strengthen ones third eye so you can experience a higher state of consciousness. Simply visit the link below the image to get started.

https://spiritualityspot.com/meditation

Contents

INTRODUCTION 1
CHAPTER ONE: WHAT IS TAI CHI? 3
    HISTORY OF TAI CHI 5
    BEGINNING OF TAI CHI 7
    MODERN TAI CHI 7
CHAPTER TWO: THE PHILOSOPHY AND BENEFITS OF TAI CHI 10
    PHILOSOPHY OF TAI CHI 10
    BENEFITS OF TAI CHI 12
    IS IT SAFE TO PRACTICE TAI CHI? 16
    DIFFERENCE BETWEEN YOGA AND TAI CHI 16
    DANTIANS 17
    LOCATIONS OF THE DANTIANS 17
    POINTS TO REMEMBER ABOUT DANTIANS 18
    RELATIONSHIP BETWEEN DANTIANS AND TAI CHI 18
CHAPTER THREE: THE FIVE STYLES: CHEN, YANG, WU, SUN, AND HAO 19
    THE STYLES 19
    HOW TO CHOOSE THE BEST TAI CHI STYLE 24
    THE STYLE FOR BEGINNERS 25
    THE STYLE FOR PEOPLE OVER FIFTY 25
CHAPTER FOUR: TAI CHI VS. QIGONG (CHI KUNG) 27
    INTRODUCTION TO QIGONG 27

THE OBJECTIVE OF QIGONG	31
DIFFERENCES	32
DIFFERENT MOVEMENTS	33

CHAPTER FIVE: TAI CHI MEDITATION AND BREATHWORK ... 35

LEARNING THE EXPERIENCE	36
THE PRACTICALITIES	37
OBSTACLES BEGINNERS OFTEN FACE	40
MULTIPLE DISTRACTIONS	41
LEARN TO STICK WITH THE ROUTINE	42
TAI CHI AND MEDITATION	43
FINDING EMPTINESS	44
TAI CHI MEDITATION TECHNIQUES	45
TAI CHI AND BREATHING	47
PERFORMING TAI CHI BREATHING	48
WHY YOU SHOULDN'T FOCUS ON TAI CHI BREATHING	49
GUIDELINES FOR TAI CHI BREATHING	50
INTEGRATING TAI CHI BREATHING INTO YOUR WORKOUT	51
WHY YOU SHOULDN'T PAY TOO MUCH ATTENTION TO BREATHING	53

CHAPTER SIX: STANCES AND FOOTWORK ... 54

TAI CHI STANCES	54
FUNDAMENTAL FOOTWORK	58

CHAPTER SEVEN: HAND MOVEMENTS ... 62

HAND POSTURES	63
TAI CHI MOVEMENTS	67

CHAPTER EIGHT: TAI CHI WARM-UP EXERCISES ... 70

WARM-UP EXERCISES	70
STRETCHING	71

CHAPTER NINE: THE 24-MOVE SEQUENCE ... 76

COMMENCING FORM	77
PARTING THE HORSE'S MANE	80
WHITE CRANE SPREADS ITS WINGS	82
PLAYING THE LUTE	84
REPULSING THE MONKEY	85
GRASPING THE BIRD'S TAIL ON THE RIGHT AND LEFT	86

- Single Whip 87
- Cloud Hands 87
- High Pat on the Horse 89
- Kick Out with the Right and Left Heel 89
- Reverse Kick 89
- Side Kick 90
- Double Punch 91
- The Serpent in the Grass on the Right, Golden Cockerel Stands on Its Left Leg 91
- Maiden Working the Shuttles 92
- Needle at the Bottom of the Sea 92
- Flash Arms Like a Fan 93
- Turn, Deflect, Parry, and Punch 93

CHAPTER TEN: PUSHING HANDS: EIGHT GATES AND FIVE STEPS 95
- Eight Gates and Five Steps 97

CHAPTER ELEVEN: COMBAT TACTICS AND SEQUENCES 99
- Focus on Timing, Movement, and Distance 99
- Understanding the Physical Strategy 99
- Land the First Hit 100
- End the Fight with Little Force 100
- Move Carefully 100
- Become Hard 101
- Throw in Some Yin and Yang 101

CHAPTER TWELVE: DAILY TAI CHI PRACTICE 102
- Tips 103

CHAPTER THIRTEEN: WHAT TO EXPECT FROM YOUR FIRST CLASS 105
- Meditative and Quiet Surroundings 105
- A Diverse Group 106
- Introduction to Tai Chi 106
- Warm-Up 106
- Breathing Exercises 107
- Stretches 107

  Instruction of Movements 107
  Repetition of Movements 108
  Relaxation and Cool Down 108
  Socialize 108
CONCLUSION 110
HERE'S ANOTHER BOOK BY MARI SILVA THAT YOU MIGHT LIKE 111
YOUR FREE GIFT (ONLY AVAILABLE FOR A LIMITED TIME) 112
REFERENCES 113

Introduction

Tai Chi is an age-old practice used to calm the mind and body. It is a sequence of different movements, postures, and forms that require you to maintain focus. Tai Chi is an internal martial art and can be used in combat. Through Tai Chi, you learn to harness your qi and the energy around you to defeat your opponent. If you have watched the movie *Mulan*, you know how she uses her qi to defeat the Huns.

Tai Chi is about using breath and other meditative techniques to relax your mind and control energy flow. You can practice its different movements while you sit, walk, stand or move. You may need to adapt the movements, so you can perform them in different situations.

If you are new to Tai Chi, you can use this book as your guide. In this book, you will first be introduced to Tai Chi to give you a brief history of this martial art. You will then look at its philosophy and principles, which are extremely important for you to know if you want to become a Tai Chi practitioner. You will then move on to how Tai Chi benefits your physical, spiritual, mental, and emotional wellbeing. There is a lot of research being conducted to determine how the art reduces the risk of developing certain illnesses and diseases, and you will look at these as well.

Since Tai Chi is an internal martial art, it focuses on breathing and meditation to help you focus and manage energy. You learn to harness your qi and use it to maintain different postures and movements. It is only when you master this that you can balance your body in any position. This book has all the information you need about Tai Chi meditation and the different techniques you can use to switch into the meditative state. You will also learn strategies and tips to defeat your opponent if you were to fight.

The book also provides information on the different movements and stances used in Tai Chi. It has instructions and illustrations to help you master the movements. Since Tai Chi is not a fun sport, it can be difficult for you to stick to it. This book has several tips you can use to help you persevere with the art and improve over time. It is best to work with people you know to maintain discipline.

Hopefully, you will learn more about Tai Chi and master the different forms and movements used. Thank you for choosing this book. You should find it informative in your quest to learn Tai Chi.

Chapter One: What is Tai Chi?

Tai Chi is an art that helps you to learn to embrace the mind, spirit, and body. This art originated in ancient China, and it is an effective exercise routine that helps you maintain the health of your body and mind. It requires a great depth of skill and knowledge to practice the art, but it is easy to learn and embrace the benefits. Most people continue to use this art throughout their lives.

There are different forms of Tai Chi, and the major ones will be discussed later in the book. Every style has a different feature, while the principles of each style remain the same. Some essential principles include the following:

- Integrating the mind with the body
- Controlling movements and breath
- Generating energy internally
- Being mindful
- Loosening the muscles
- Being serene

The objective of Tai Chi is to help you cultivate the life energy or qi found within the human body to make sure the energy flows powerfully and smoothly throughout the body. It is only possible to maintain total harmony between the outer and inner selves by integrating the body and mind. You can maintain this balance by empowering yourself through the practice of qi. There are modern Tai Chi programs that incorporate medical science, and these programs will deliver benefits faster.

There is much more to Tai Chi than one may initially believe. Not many understand the art because they cannot describe it easily in a sentence. This art is enjoyable, aesthetically pleasing, and easy to practice. Tai Chi is part meditation and part-integral exercise for the parts of the mind and body. This art can help you think clearly but bear in mind that it can be a different experience for you. It is best to practice the art regularly if you want to benefit from it to the maximum.

When you perform Tai Chi, you realize that every flowing movement you make has immense inner strength. The movements are like the water in a river. Beneath the surface of the river, there is an underlying current, which has immense power. This power can heal you and improve your wellbeing. When you practice Tai Chi consistently, you will feel the internal energy and learn to convert that energy into an internal force that allows you to generate more internal energy. This process enhances the development of Tai Chi, which leads to a balanced physical and mental state. Your balance and agility also improve. Tai Chi focuses on helping you build inner strength. This means you can begin practicing Tai Chi at any age.

Research shows that Tai Chi improves flexibility, immunity, strength, and fitness, relieves pain, and increases your wellbeing. You will look at these benefits in detail in the subsequent chapter. Your muscles need to become strong if you want to protect and support your joints. Strong muscles are also important to maintain normal physical function. Through flexibility exercises, you will move easily and improve the circulation of blood and fluid throughout your body. This improves healing. You also need to be fit if you want to maintain the health of your muscles, heart, and lungs. Movements in Tai Chi ensure you transfer weight equally from one part of your body to another, enabling you to maintain balance.

Tai Chi is more than the health benefits it has to offer. It is extremely easy to learn, and most people who practice Tai Chi make it a way of life. Since Tai Chi is a very deep subject, there is nobody who knows everything about Tai Chi. The subject is fascinating, and many want to embark on the journey. When you practice Tai Chi, you enter a state of tranquility and move into a different space, world, and time. You do not have to hustle or maintain a schedule in this world. This is a spiritual experience. These types of experiences are satisfying beyond words.

History of Tai Chi

The story of Tai Chi starts with Buddha. It begins with the beginning of Zen and ancient old times in 600 BC. Jia Ye was the only person who knew why Buddha picked up a lotus flower during a meeting and smiled at everyone. He was a great disciple and smiled back at Buddha because he understood the meaning. This was when Buddha told everybody on Mount Lengjia, "I have a treasure, like a secret mountain, which is real but with not any appearance, now I give it to JiaYe the Great." The treasure was to be passed between people, which was the case when families passed the treasure and learning of Zen from one generation to the next.

Buddhism in India began to decay after the Zen was passed on to the DaMo, which was the tenth generation. So, DaMo went to China during the Liang dynasty. He went to the Shao-Lin temple and settled down there. The Emperor of the Liang dynasty went to meet DaMo. It was then that DaMo developed methods of training that helped people develop inner peace. He trained a person's soul and body. Another one of his contributions was the development of another form of fighting called Shao-Lin Kung Fu. This is where the student learns to fight using his spirit. Shao-Lin Kung Fu led to the beginning of the Tang dynasty.

One of the founders of Taoism, Lao-Tzu, was alive at the same time as Buddha. Lao-Tzu was a famous Chinese philosopher, and he developed the theory of Yin and Yang. When he developed this theory, he described the relationship between nature and man. He also talked about the relationship between the strong and weak. Confucius once said he was a dragon. His paper "Tao-Te Ching" was valued greatly by people for many years. In this paper, he talked about how one should learn from nature since nature is everybody's first teacher. He also said, "The newborn baby is weak and soft, but the growing force is strong. When he grows up, he becomes strong and stiff, and the life strength is weak and soft. When something is overwhelmed, it is near its end, although it looks strong." These words have influenced Tai Chi since it is close to Taoism. After Lao-Tzu developed this form of Tai Chi, there were numerous training methods developed in China that aimed to combine the forces of nature and people.

There were different forms of physical practices used in China, and in each of these styles, many people, including Wang Chongyang in Zhongnan Mountain, Xu Xuanping in the Sung Dynasty, and Chang Sanfeng, the founder of Tai-Chi Chuan, learned everything they needed to from nature. They learned to pay attention to every thought and breath. They also focused on how their minds began to change. They learned from outer appearances and learned the meaning of the different natural phenomena.

India Yoga school methods, Taoism methods, and Buddhism methods used traditional and oriental training styles, which are different from modern learning methods. These skills are different from bodybuilding and jogging. These forms of exercise are easy ways to solve different problems in life.

Beginning of Tai Chi

Chinese Kung Fu was developed and created in the Buddhism temple called Shao-Lin. This was where most people went to learn Kung Fu. Chang Sanfeng also learned Kung Fu in this temple before traveling across China to learn more about Taoism. He settled down in the Wudang Mountains. Since he was a recluse and a well-respected master, many people went to him to learn martial arts. This form of martial arts is termed Wudang Chuan. Shao-Lin and Wudang are the major forms of Kung Fu styles. One of these forms, the Wudang form, is a form of inner Kung Fu.

Wudang began Tai Chi in his later years, and he did not teach this skill publicly. It was an esoteric technique that was passed on from one generation to the next. Some Tai Chi skills were passed on, but most of them were left unknown to the public.

Modern Tai Chi

Modern Tai Chi began close to 400 years ago. Now you will look at a few styles that developed during this phase.

Chen School of Tai Chi

After the Ming dynasty fell and decayed over time, Chen Wangting moved back to his village. He began to study the art of Kung Fu. Since he was a warrior and general, he was closely connected with Shao-Lin. This allowed him to learn more about the various styles of Kung Fu. He knew the different methods and theories used in this form of martial arts. He compiled and developed a version of Kung Fu in his village, which focused only on inner values and peace.

Wang School of Tai Chi

Wang Zongyue developed this style of Tai Chi. He was a recluse in his village and theorized various aspects of Tai Chi. People believed that Wang carried the skill of Tai Chi, which was a gift given to him by Chang Sanfeng. He was very skilled at fighting and taught children how to defend themselves. Some historians theorized that Wang taught the theory of Tai Chi to the people in Chen's village. He passed on different forms of martial arts, including Tai Chi, to the people in Chen's village. It was only 60 years after his death that his paper on Tai Chi was discovered in Wuyang County. This led to the development of the Wushi Tai Chi school.

Chen's School to Yang's School of Tai Chi

Yang LuChan, one of the greatest masters of Tai Chi, had gone to Chen's village to learn this martial art when he was young. Since the skill was kept a secret by the people in the village, he pretended to be a beggar. He used to learn martial arts in secret when he worked in the village. When the people in the village discovered what he was doing, they convinced the head of the village to change the rules. They allowed people from other parts of China to come to the village to learn more about this skill.

Wushi School of Tai Chi

Wushi Xiang was a rich landlord. He preferred Kung Fu and practiced this art regularly. He was amicable and made friends easily. Wushi befriended Yang when he came back from Chen's village. Since Wushi loved martial arts, he admired Yang's movements, but he could not learn everything from Yang. Wushi then went to Chen's village to learn the art of Tai Chi. Because the head of the village had died, not many people in the village taught the art of Tai Chi. He then wandered until he came across a member from Chen's village, Chen ChingPing, who taught the skill there. Wu also learned the art of Tai Chi from the paper written by Wang. This was published when it was found in the salt shop.

Wu School of Tai Chi

The Wu style was developed by Wu Quanyou, one of the Imperial Guard members during the Ching dynasty. Wu had mastered Kung Fu before he learned the art of Tai Chi. Wu took care of Yang Luchan when he fell ill because he respected the skill. Since

Wu took care of Yang, they became good friends, and Yang was indebted to Wu. Yang taught Wu the skill of Tai Chi in return for his favor. After his death, Yang asked his son Yang Banhou to teach Wu. When he mastered the art of Tai Chi, he used his understanding of both Kung Fu and Tai Chi to develop a new style that became known as Wu. His style is slow, soft, and calm. The style required people to pay attention to their movements to help them improve their condition.

Chapter Two: The Philosophy and Benefits of Tai Chi

Philosophy of Tai Chi

The roots of Tai Chi lie in the Chinese way of life and philosophy, whereas Confucianism and Taoism were the responses to philosophical, social, and political conditions in ancient China. Taoism focused on your mystical and individualistic character and how nature influences this character. Confucianism, on the other hand, is also concerned with human society and social issues.

Millions of people followed the thought patterns defined by Confucius. Most experts are surprised at this since this is one rule many people have followed. Confucius had one goal: to restore order and peace in all provinces. He believed that everybody needed to follow traditional values and follow traditional rules and paths to bring order and peace to their province. He also believed that people understood hierarchy and the order of earth and heaven.

The principles of Taoism lie in the idea that Tao (or the Way) is the reason why everything that is material in the world changes. This is the universal fundamental principle of any change that happens in the world.

You can translate the Tao Te Ching into the Law of Virtue and the path you need to take to abide by it. It became easier for people to put the philosophy of Tao into action when they began to perform and understand Tai Chi. According to Lao Tzu, you should never put yourself against the way things should be. It is important never to try to force the flow of events to change. When you act naturally and let things happen the way they should, you find harmony in your essence. This essence is called the Tao. The idea of the Tao is that the One was born from it. An example of the philosophy of Tai Chi is the story of the Tai Chi master, the emperor, and the bird.

The forces of both the yin and yang came into being when the one created the two. These forces of nature are the opposite of each other. They were also locked in a struggle that is extremely difficult for either of them to win. When one of these forces reached the top, the other found a way to move to the top as well. If you want to live in harmony with Tao, you need to live according to these forces of nature. You also need to maintain an approach in life that is non-interfering.

Maleness represents yang — the light, heat, sun, day, and heaven. On the other hand, yin represents femininity, such as darkness, cold, night, and the moon. All phenomena have these opposite states in them, and these states are termed as the presence in the absence.

Tai Chi uses the principles of Confucianism and Taoism. When you practice Tai Chi, it offers you an outlet for both. China cares about personal defense. The elements of self-improvement and physical action can help you strengthen your mind and body. Most instructors show their students how they should use Tai Chi to resolve the tension in their bodies. They also show their students how to perform inward reflex and outward actions. These movements are central to maintain balance in your body. Here are a couple of points to remember:

- Everything you do and any activity you perform is always a part of the whole
- Any activity you perform includes chi, yin, and yang
- Change is the only constant thing in your life
- Do not force your body into moving; let the movements occur naturally
- Your yin and yang will constantly change
- Be gentle with your body if you want to be strong

Benefits of Tai Chi

Now that you know the Tai Chi philosophy, it is worth looking at some of the benefits.

Reduces Stress

While there is only anecdotal evidence available to confirm that Tai Chi reduces stress, people choose to learn Tai Chi to reduce anxiety. In a study conducted by Zheng et al. (2018), the researchers compared the effects of traditional exercise and Tai Chi on stress. The study was conducted on fifty subjects, and it was noted that Tai Chi and traditional exercise provided the same benefits to help people manage anxiety.

Since Tai Chi also uses focused breathing techniques and meditation, the researchers noted that Tai Chi is more effective than traditional forms of exercise to reduce stress. However, more research is needed to corroborate this.

Unlike some forms of traditional exercise, Tai Chi has a lower impact on the muscles and joints. It is also accessible and easy to perform. Researchers found that Tai Chi is inexpensive and safe. If you experience stress-related anxiety and are healthy, it may be a good idea to choose Tai Chi.

Improves Your Mood

Tai Chi can improve your mood if you are anxious or depressed. A study conducted by Yeung et al. (2017) concluded that Tai Chi, if practiced regularly, could reduce the symptoms of depression and anxiety. Experts believe that mindful, slow movements and breaths affect the central nervous system positively. These activities also regulate mood hormones. Research is being conducted to determine the link between improved mood and Tai Chi.

Better Sleep Cycle

If you want to improve your sleep cycle, you should practice Tai Chi regularly. A study was conducted by Caldwell et al. (2016) for ten weeks on young adults with depression and anxiety. The researchers found that the subjects who practiced Tai Chi regularly found their sleep had improved compared to those who did not. The subjects who practiced Tai Chi also experienced fewer anxiety and depression symptoms. A study conducted by Chan et al. in 2016 showed that older adults could also use Tai Chi to improve their sleep. Researchers found that adults who practiced Tai Chi twice a week for two months slept better than those who did not practice it.

Aids in Weight Loss

If you practice Tai Chi regularly, it can help with weight loss. A study was conducted by Hui, S. et al (2015) to determine how Tai Chi reduces weight. The subjects in the study were older people who practiced Tai Chi for forty-five minutes, five times a week. The researchers noted the weight of the subjects regularly and tracked it for twelve weeks. At the end of the study, they noted that the adults lost over a pound without any changes to their lifestyle.

Improves Cognition

Research shows that Tai Chi can improve cognition, especially in those who have shown signs of cognitive impairment. Tai Chi also increases the ease with which a person can perform any activities. It can also help to improve a person's memory and ability to carry out complex tasks.

Reduces the Risk of Falling

When you do Tai Chi, you need to perform movements that require you to maintain balance. A study conducted by Mortazavi et al. (2018) showed that older adults who perform Tai Chi are not afraid of falling because they know they can control their bodies. Tai Chi also helps to reduce actual falls after a few weeks of practicing Tai Chi. When you are afraid of falling, it reduces the quality of your life and independence. These falls can lead to complications. Studies also showed that Tai Chi improves your wellbeing and quality of life.

Reduces the Symptoms of Fibromyalgia

Experts state that performing Tai Chi helps you to manage and reduce the symptoms of chronic disease. Tai Chi also compliments some traditional pain management methods. A study conducted by Wang et al. (2018) showed that Tai Chi helped reduce several fibromyalgia symptoms. The subjects were asked to participate in Tai Chi for a year. At the end of the study, the researchers noted that participants showed fewer fibromyalgia symptoms than other participants.

Improves Chronic Obstructive Pulmonary Disease (COPD) Symptoms

Research shows that Tai Chi helps to reduce the symptoms of COPD. A study conducted by Wu et al. (2014) on subjects with COPD showed that these subjects could perform exercise easily. These subjects also reported that their lives had improved since they began Tai Chi.

Reduces the Symptoms of Parkinson's Disease

A controlled and randomized trial performed by Li et al. (2012) on 195 subjects showed that Tai Chi helped to reduce the symptoms of Parkinson's disease. People with Parkinson's may regain their balance and become stronger. During the trial, the researchers found that people with the disease did not fall as often as those who did not practice Tai Chi. The art also helps you increase overall balance and leg strength.

It's Safe for People with Heart Disease

If you have heart disease, it is best to perform Tai Chi since it is a light or moderate exercise. If you do have cardiovascular disease, you should practice Tai Chi for the following reasons:

- It makes you physically active
- It becomes easy to lose weight
- It improves the quality of your life

Reduces Pain from Arthritis

A small-scale trial was conducted by Uhlig et al. (2010) with only fifteen subjects. These subjects had rheumatoid arthritis and practiced the art for twelve weeks. The researchers checked in with the subjects at regular intervals and noted that the subjects reported improved balance and mobility and less pain.

Another study was conducted by Wang et al. (2009) on a large scale with forty subjects. These subjects had knee osteoarthritis. They practiced Tai Chi twice a week for twelve weeks. Each session lasted for 60 minutes. At the end of the study, the researchers noted that the subjects showed improved quality of life and mobility. They also found that the subjects reported less pain.

Experts recommend performing Tai Chi instead of undergoing physical therapy since the former is more effective when treating knee osteoarthritis. You must ensure that you speak to your doctor before you begin with Tai Chi. Your doctor can give you a modified version of the movements.

Is it Safe to Practice Tai Chi?

Tai Chi does not have too many side effects since it is considered a safe exercise. If you are a beginner, you may experience aches or pains when you practice it for the first time. Rigorous and difficult forms of Tai Chi can lead to injury. If you do not practice Tai Chi carefully, it may lead to injuries. It is best to find an instructor or join a class if you are new to Tai Chi and want to reduce the potential of any injury. Do not perform Tai Chi if you are pregnant. If you have been performing Tai Chi while pregnant, you need to speak to your doctor to see if it is safe to continue.

Tai Chi focuses on exact movements and posture. It is difficult to learn these on your own, so it is best to take a class or work with an instructor if you are new to Tai Chi. This art is taught all over the United States and other countries. It is best to find something close to your home.

Difference Between Yoga and Tai Chi

Tai Chi is an art that uses fluid movements. As mentioned earlier, this art originated in China, while yoga originated in India, and it focuses on poses and maintaining your breath. Both yoga and Tai Chi are exercise forms that involve deep breathing and meditation and have the following benefits:

- Improves sleep
- Relieves stress
- Improves mood

Dantians

In this section, you will look at the dantians or the energy centers in your body. There are three dantians in the body, and you use each of them when performing Tai Chi. These energy centers in the body control and store both the energy potential and energy in the body. These centers are also termed the three treasures.

Locations of the Dantians

Now, look at where each of these is in the body.

Lower Dantian

The lower dantian, also known as the jing, is found two or three inches below the belly button. This is the source of all energy that will build in the physical body. It allows you to develop the energy and use your shen and qi.

Middle Dantian

The middle dantian, also called qi, is found in the heart. This energy is created from air and food. It is closely related to your thoughts and emotions.

Upper Dantian

The upper dantian or shen is found at the center between your eyebrows. It can be a little higher and is closely related to your consciousness and spirit.

Concerning dantians in Tai Chi, this book will often refer to the lower dantian. Only when a distinction is made are the other dantians considered. A few reasons for considering only the lower dantian are:

- This is the original and first source of energy or chi in the body

- You cannot feel the other Tai Chi energy points or dantians in the body until there is enough energy in your body. The energy from the lower dantian travels to these parts of the body and lends them some feeling or sensation
- This dantian is the center of all your power

Points to Remember About Dantians

The goal in performing any Tai Chi or Qigong movements is to build the body's energy and increase the circulation of different body fluids, including blood, within the body. You can increase your energy in the dantians easily. You can increase the energy in the dantians and clean the energy if you maintain good posture and breathe freely. The following are a few ways you can increase the energy:

- Maintain good posture
- Improve breathing
- Move the energy from the dantians to other parts of the body
- Coordinate the movements you make with your breath

Relationship Between Dantians and Tai Chi

Tai Chi is an art developed and created very smartly. Every movement you make in Tai Chi is carefully designed. The movements help you build and activate the different energy centers in your body. The creators of Tai Chi developed these movements based on thousands of years of research and refinement. If you are a beginner, you will reap the benefits of Tai Chi from the knowledge learned from your teacher. When you perform any movement in Tai Chi, you learn to let the energy flow through the dantians to the rest of your body. You will look at the importance of the lower dantian in Tai Chi breathing and explain how you need to use it to improve your movements.

Chapter Three: The Five Styles: Chen, Yang, Wu, Sun, and Hao

This chapter will provide you with information on the different styles of Tai Chi. You will also learn how you can choose the right style for you.

The Styles

Chen Style

In the year 1670, a descendant of the Chen family, Chen Wangting, developed different Tai Chi routines based on the classical Chen style of Tai Chi. This form is practiced today by many people across China and other parts of the world. Wangting was influenced by different schools of other arts, such as boxing. Qi Jiguang, a member of the Imperial Army, also influenced him. Wangting used the book written by Jiguang. Wangting also assimilated various techniques of Tuna and Daoyin into his routines. When combined with the use of consciousness and clarity, these techniques led to the development and practice of Taoism.

Tuna and Daovin are very different from each other. The former focuses on breathing and calming exercises, while the latter focuses on exerting inner forces. Several Tai Chi styles also use Qigong exercises that developed from Tuna. Wangting also used aspects of traditional Chinese medicine (TCM). When he combined these styles, the Tai Chi developed by him became a system of exercises that focused on different actions, mental concentration, and breathing. These forms are closely connected. This led to the development of a new style of Tai Chi, which improved all forms of health. When Wangting developed this style of Tai Chi, he did not let any other parts of China know about this style. The clan was very close-knit, and they never taught anybody who would leave the village this style. They did not teach their daughters but taught their daughters-in-law this style of Tai Chi since the former would leave the village.

Another member of the Chen family, Chen Xin, illustrated the art and wrote a book about the Chen style of Tai Chi in his later years. In his book, he talked about the proper movements and postures that one must maintain when they practice Tai Chi. He also explained the medical and philosophical background of every movement and routine. This book was only published in China in 1932. Chen Changxing's grandson, Chen Fake, popularized the Chen style of Tai Chi when he taught people in the Chen village.

Chen Fake was from the Chen family, and he was from the seventeenth generation. He was probably the greatest leader and the most accomplished member of the Chen family. There are numerous stories told in China about his prowess and knowledge in Tai Chi. He was well liked by everybody and made no enemies for as long as he lived in Beijing. He was well known for his perfect disposition.

Chen Fake was the youngest member of the Chen family and was born when his father was around 65 years old. Since Fake's brothers had died because of an epidemic, everybody around him spoiled him, and no one forced him to do the things that he should have done. He was a weakling since he refused to practice Tai Chi. Chen Fake knew his health would improve if he practiced Tai Chi, but he was lazy. He never bothered to practice it, and he soon became a laughingstock in his village. His father was well known for his skill in Tai Chi.

When Fake grew older, he felt ashamed of himself. He did not like how people talked about him and always felt he was letting his father and family down. His cousin was known for his skills. Fake decided to catch up to his cousin and beat him in the art. Since his cousin practiced every day, he continued to improve. Fake practiced every day, but he could not perform the art as well as his cousin. Fake's cousin was strong and an expert in Tai Chi, so Fake began to worry that he could never be as good as his cousin.

One day Chen Fake and his cousin were walking back from their practice in the fields. On their way back, his cousin remembered that he had left something back in the field. He mentioned to Fake that he should run back and bring the item. He also told Fake he would walk slowly so that Fake could catch up with him on his return. When Fake ran toward his cousin, he suddenly realized that he could beat his cousin if he practiced hard. After this realization, he began to practice harder every day. He improved in strength and technique, and he eventually beat his cousin. Since Fake's father was away from home for about three years, nobody could attribute his improvement to his training. Fake's improvement was a direct result of the time he spent practicing every movement and flow.

During his years in Beijing, Chen Fake met and taught thousands of students. Most of his students performed this style of Tai Chi to cure a specific illness or improve their health. A few of Chen's famous students include Li Zhongyiun, Hong Junsheng, Li Jinwu, Tang Hao, Lei Mumin, Feng Zhiqiang, Gu Liuxin, Liu Rui Zhang, and Tian Xiuchen. This style of Tai Chi is characterized using spiritual forces. The movements in this style are like other forms of martial arts. It is a mix of fast and hard movements along with soft and slow movements. The style has a mix of low and powerful stances. The Chen style of

Tai Chi is used in combat. The movements are effective and practical, which makes them suitable for the young.

Yang Style

This is the most popular form or style of Tai Chi. Yang Lu-Chan created it during the period 1799 to 1872. Yang had always loved martial arts, and he studied different forms of these arts since he was a child. He also studied with different masters. He used to spar with people from different villages and lost once to a descendent or member of the Chen village. He was impressed by the opponent's form and movements. He had never come across someone who used soft, powerful, and curve-like movements while performing martial arts. He had always learned the hard styles of martial arts.

Yang wanted to learn this soft art. He was quite desperate, so he pretended to faint outside his opponent's house. He acted like a beggar. Yang started to wake up every night and peep into the room where the villagers practiced this art. He mirrored the movements performed by the villagers and soon became a skilled practitioner. When the Chen elders caught Yang, they could have had him executed for his behavior. But the elders were impressed with his skill and took him in as a student.

Yang then left the village and traveled around China to spread awareness of the art. Since there was nobody who could defeat him, he was termed "Yang the invincible." He soon developed his style and taught people he met that same style. He also taught many members of the Imperial Court. This style of Tai Chi is characterized by slow, graceful, and gentle movements. It is easy for anybody to perform these movements. This style also promotes health, and this has become popular these days.

Hao or Wu Style

It is important to note that this Wu style is different from the Wu style discussed in the next section. Many words in Mandarin sound the same but have different meanings. These words are called Pinyins.

This style of Tai Chi is also known as Hao. This style was first created by Wu Yuxiang between the years 1812 and 1880. He then passed on this style to Hao Weizheng, who developed the style and added his flair to it between 1849 and 1920. This style is not practiced commonly, and the people who created it studied the Chen and Yang styles of Tai Chi.

Hao is a style of Tai Chi that is characterized by internally slow and loose movements. These movements are close-knit when it comes to the outward experience. In this style of Tai Chi, you need to maintain the right position. The internal power in your body controls any external movement you make. When you look at the higher levels of this style, it will appear more rounded and larger.

Wu Style

The Wu style of Tai Chi was developed between the period 1834 and 1942. It was first introduced by Wu Quan-you and later by his son Wu Jian-Quan. This form of Tai Chi emphasizes the incoming force and the softness placed on the movements. This style is rich in movements and focuses on hand movements and techniques. This style requires you to maintain a leaning posture. This is a pleasant style of Tai Chi and has depth.

Sun Style

The Sun style is the youngest form of Tai Chi and is quite recent. It was created between the period 1861 and 1932 by Sun Lu-tang. Before he learned the art of Tai Chi, he learned two other forms of internal styles of martial arts known as Baguaguan and Xingyiguan. In the year 1912, Sun ran into the creator of the Hao style of Tai Chi. Hao was sick at the time, and Sun took care of Hao. He did not know who Hao was and did his best to find him the right doctor and a hotel for him to stay at. When Hao recovered, he taught Sun Tai Chi.

Sun created his version of Tai Chi based on the Hao style, but he made sure the movements were based on agile steps. When one foot moved either forward or backward, the other foot would also need to move in the same direction. The movements are like a river, and they flow smoothly. There is a powerful exercise that you need to perform every time you change directions. The Sun style of Tai Chi has higher stances.

The exercise performed in the Sun style of Tai Chi is known as Qigong and improves your internal strength. This power is effective when it comes to relaxing and healing. Since the style uses higher stances, it is extremely easy for older people to perform. The style is also compact, which means you do not require a large space to perform the movements. The Sun style of Tai Chi has a lot of depth, and it will hold your interest if you choose to learn it.

How to Choose the Best Tai Chi Style

As discussed earlier, there are five styles of Tai Chi. You can modify and improve the style to suit your fitness levels and goals. All Tai Chi styles ensure you move from one movement to the next easily. The following are a few points to keep in mind when you choose the right style for you:

- The yang chi style focuses on graceful and slow movements. Every move you make will relax you, which is a great point to start with if you are a beginner.

- The Wu style is practiced extremely slowly, and it emphasizes the smaller movements you make.

- The Chen style uses both fast and slow movements, and it may be difficult for you to perform this style of Tai Chi if you are very new to this art.

- The Sun style is like the Chen style, but unlike the Chen style, the Sun style involves less punching, crouching, and kicking. This means it does not demand much from your body.

- The Hao style is not practiced by many people since it is not commonly known. This style focuses more on your internal strength and the accurate positioning of the limbs.

The Style for Beginners

If you find one style more comfortable or can perform the movements easily, you will likely learn to finish it. You will also remember the order movements and can practice the style with ease. You will need to follow the steps below when you want to choose a style:

- It is easy to learn the Wu, Hao, and Yang styles since the physical coordination needed to perform these skills is easy. These styles are easier than the Chen style.

- If your body is tight and you have trouble stretching, you need to stick to the larger Tai Chi styles. It is only through these styles that you can perform the movements easily over time. Your muscles will loosen over time even if you perform the smaller styles of Tai Chi.

- If you have injured knees or a bad lower back, do not perform Tai Chi styles with lower stances since these strain your back. Use smaller styles of Tai Chi if you want a higher stance.

- Large Tai Chi styles improve your leg strength since they have deeper and longer stances.

- The smaller Tai Chi styles are easy since you can easily perform the style's internal work. This is the easiest way to work with the internal organs.

The Style for People Over Fifty

Since the short-form and slow-motion styles of Tai Chi are the easiest to learn, it is best for people over fifty to practice these styles. If you are over fifty and want to learn a long form, it is best to start with a short form since this will help loosen your muscles. You will learn the art easily and absorb, remember, and enjoy the Tai Chi style you have chosen. Styles of Tai Chi that include longer and deeper stances can affect your back and knees. If you are strong, you can take longer and deeper stances at the usual speed. Small styles of Tai Chi, such as Wu, are often the best choice to improve the health of your organs. For people over fifty, it is difficult to make large movements.

Chapter Four: Tai Chi vs. Qigong (Chi Kung)

Introduction to Qigong

Qigong literally translates to work using energy. This is an old form of yoga developed in Asia. It has been around for many years, and this exercise is performed using standing movements. You can also perform this exercise by sitting down. There are different Qigong systems, which you can use to improve the way you work with your breath. These Qigong forms have come from different parts of the world, and each form focuses on one aspect. Most of these forms focus on health, while others focus on martial arts.

The systems in your body work on harnessing this power to help you learn to channel your energy through your palms. Most health practitioners in ancient times used to channel this energy to heal their patients. You can do this easily if you learn to focus better on the systems. Some different monasteries and temples focus on the depth and spiritual cultivation of medication. Some forms involve the use of movements, while others are based on visualization. All these forms use specialized breathing while you continue to perform the activity on hand. The principle that guides these practices focuses on coordinating the body's movements and eyes, your breath, the focus of your mind, and more. If you want to perform non-movement and passive exercises, you need to focus on your inward vision. You also learn to explore different inner realms when you let your breath guide you.

Now this book will take the time to explain this formula better. It will dissect it so that you can understand each detail. The objective of Qigong is to coordinate between these aspects. Consider the following if you want Qigong to be effective.

Eyes in Qigong

When it comes to Western civilization, the eyes are termed as the gateway to your soul. According to Taoism, the eyes are used to guide the spirit or the shen. It is believed that the energy in the body follows the spirit while the body fluids, including blood, will follow the qi.

The eyes in your body work as the command center. You can use your eyes to manage the energy in the body. Your eyes also help you control the flow of energy in the body. When you master this, you can learn to project the energy outward and influence your environment.

Body Movements in Qigong

The body movements in Qigong follow a sequence, and each sequence has a different set of exercises. Every exercise in the sequence uses the different energy meridians or pathways that are present in your body. Through these exercises, you learn to trace the edges in the energy fields in your body. You also learn to embrace and smoothen the body's energy fields to help you manage the potency of the flow of energy through your body. These movements involve the use of different degrees of energy and exertion. The exercises can be rigorous if you are a beginner.

If you want to learn more about how this works, read the story of the Shaolin temple and Bodhidharma. Bodhi created a routine known as the Eighteen Hands of Lohan. When this routine is mixed with Kung Fu, you may exert yourself. This form of martial arts is more like yoga. You can hold static postures or emphasize the flow of energy and the continuity of motion.

Mental Focus in Qigong

This is an important aspect of Qigong and its practice. Most students overlook this art of breathing. If you want to master Qigong, you need to pay close attention to every critical energy component in your body. Qigong also engages in the energy stored in the heart. This energy is mapped to the fire element. The energy in the heart works with the spirit. Experts believe that the link between intention and attention will help you master life. In Qigong, you need to focus on different body movements and learn to track them with your eyes. To do this, you need to focus your mind and learn to be in the present. The reward of this process is immense. You also learn to draw on the energy from the earth.

Use of Breath in Qigong

Your breath circulates in your body through different meridians. This is the energy from the air, and it combines with the qi from the food you consume to produce energy in your body. It is the coordination between attention and body movements that open blockages and free the pathways. In Qigong, you learn to use your breath to gather and store it as energy in different reservoirs, known as dantians, in your body. You also learn to push the energy through different pathways in your body. If you are a beginner, you need to make an effort to learn how to extract energy from the air through your breath.

This may seem simple, but this framework will set a precedent for the energy and magic you use in Qigong. There is a lot of information you need to learn about the different movements in Qigong. Learning as much as you can is the only way to learn everything there is to know about your body's energy paths and how the energy affects you. Even if you do not understand the mechanics but learn everything about the coordinated thoughts, movements, and breathing, you will be ahead of your game.

The subject of these pathways is very new to people, and you will learn more about them in this chapter. You will look at the different mechanisms of action and understand them better. You will also learn about your intellect and how you can engage it through intention and attention. When you activate the vertical axis of your soul, you activate the energies of fire, water, and earth. You will finally unlock the first hints of the potential in your body. It is only when you do this that you can make powerful changes in your body.

The vertical axis in your body will give you the necessary spiritual and mental alignment to help you connect easily with your body. You need to do this while you practice Qigong. When you connect different aspects of yourself through the practice of Qigong, you learn to snap out of the area of wants and needs. When you learn to divert your body's energy from the harmful and wasteful patterns, you learn to connect with the energy. You also learn to accumulate and gather the power in your reservoir and use this energy as a buffer to help you overcome fatigue, disease, and lack of energy. When I say storing or accumulating energy and power, you need to create places to condense and refine the energy quality that flows through you. You can condense the energy to nourish your being and refine it, so it helps to illuminate your spirit.

You need to be extremely careful when it comes to your views on this aspect. Do not look at it in terms of capitalism—since this changes your understanding of the art. Your outlook on the energy in your body changes how you approach life. You never require too much energy in your body since there is always enough energy present in the universe. All the energy in the body and who you will be is in the present moment and is changeable.

It is extremely important for you to learn how to acquire energy from the universe. Before you acquire energy, you need to learn where this energy comes from. You cannot draw the energy from an outside source, like a river or well. The force of the universe and the energy is flowing through you every minute. It flows through every organ in your body, and the blocks you create in your being that lead to the sense of lacking since the energy stops flowing easily through your body. When you channel this imbalanced energy through your body and into your shadows, you close off your mind. You let it limit your energy and change the definition of who you are. You are also exhausted.

The Objective of Qigong

When it comes to Qigong, you do not focus on adding anything to your body. It is mostly about the removal of negative energy. When you learn to get more out of your practice, you learn to let the universal energy flow into your body. You learn to use the energy from the universe and become an agent of its will. It is only when you do this that you take your rightful place. By rightful place, this does not mean you will need to focus on far-off achievements; you will learn to live in the present.

Through Qigong, you learn to wake up and live in the current moment. You learn to take part in the present. This is an important aspect to consider when you want to eliminate any unwanted energies in your body. You remove the frustration, grief, and anger in your horizontal axis. Your horizontal soul is closely related to the falling and rising trends of your emotional and mental upheavals. This upheaval is closely tied to your life. Learn to focus on this process and focus on balancing these axes.

People often find themselves stuck at this stage since they repress most of their emotions and needs in their shadows. Most people suffer and cling to things that do not matter because of the energy they get from wood and metal. The former energy is your desire for more, while the latter is the energy to let go of things. Most people continue to hold on to negativity, and the energy in the body is imbalanced. This imbalance leads to the creation of monsters in the body.

According to traditional Chinese medicine, the lungs are important since they represent the metal element. The energy from these elements moves naturally. The liver represents energy from wood, which is naturally found. The lungs are above the liver in the body, and the essence of life is dependent on the maintenance and management of the dynamic tension and flow of energy. The body needs to maintain the inverted forces of energy. The energy from the lungs is pushed down, while the energy from the liver is pushed upward. When you die, the energy from the liver moves to heaven while the energy from the lungs moves into the earth. It is important to check the dynamic tension between these forms of energy. If you do not manage it, the energy will separate and perish.

People's lives run smoother when they learn to maintain the flow of energy in the body. You need to harmonize the flow of the energy on the horizontal axis since this helps you plug into the power of the energy on the vertical axis. The alignment of intention and attention is something you need to understand. It is only when you understand this that you can understand your condition. Do not run away from your innermost thoughts and emotions. You need to be more aware, engaged, and live in the moment.

Differences

Now that you know what Qigong is look at a few differences between Tai Chi and Qigong.

Tai Chi is One Form of Qigong

Qigong forms the basics of Tai Chi. You focus on your mind and breath in Qigong and do the same in Tai Chi. You can only maintain this focus when you master the art of Qigong.

Qigong focuses on healing and wellness, while Tai Chi is a martial art.

Qigong uses different exercises for healing. Tai Chi, on the other hand, does not focus on healing. Many people practice different forms of Tai Chi for healing and wellbeing. Qigong does not focus on any attack, fighting, or defense movements like Tai Chi does. The various Qigong movements can improve your self-defense techniques and power, especially if you practice Kung Fu or Tai Chi.

Different Movements

Qigong does not use many standing movements. You can perform Qigong while lying or sitting down. Tai Chi focuses on standing movements. Both Tai Chi and Qigong focus on careful and slow movements in general.

They Use Qi Differently

There are different exercises in Qigong, which focus or use Qi differently. This is especially true when it comes to medical Qigong. In Tai Chi, the movements do not do this. The movements in Tai Chi use whole-body movements and functions. Each of these movements uses qi differently.

The Difference in Complexity of Movement

From the previous section, you know the movements used in Qigong are simple. Tai Chi, on the other hand, uses many complex stances and movements.

Qigong Does Not Have Forms

From the previous chapter, you know there are different forms of Tai Chi. Qigong, on the other hand, only uses one form. It is only based on a series of structures of exercises. You can tailor these exercises based on your health. You can also perform these exercises whenever you want to.

Qigong is Easier than Tai Chi

A few stances and movements in Tai Chi are difficult to perform. If you have any injury or physical restriction, it may be easier for you to perform Qigong. Since Qigong uses free movements, it is easier for you to adapt to this form of martial arts. You can modify the movements in Qigong to suit your abilities and needs.

Chapter Five: Tai Chi Meditation and Breathwork

If you are a beginner, you may find the idea of sitting quietly in a room a little strange. It is hard to sit with your innermost feelings and thoughts. You may find it hard to sit and do absolutely nothing. Your mind will completely resist this. Meditation can feel alien to you if you are a beginner. It may also feel daunting, but this is fine. Meditation is a practice people have followed for over 3,000 years.

You may want to start meditating for different reasons. You probably want to feel less stressed, focus more, or be less reactive. Meditation may also be a part of personal development. You can choose to meditate to improve your relationship with the people around you. Regardless of what the reason is, you need to train your mind to become more aware. This is one of the easiest ways for you to change your perception of life.

You experience everything through your mind. Your perception of life may change dramatically when you begin to meditate. You may be inspired to meditate, but thinking about meditating is different from doing it. You will only reap the benefits of meditation when you begin practicing it. It is important to develop a regular practice, too. Before you meditate, make sure your mind is calm. Learn to understand its untamed behavior. Meditation is extremely simple; however, you need to keep a few points in mind before you start.

Learning the Experience

If you are a beginner, it is best to use guided meditation techniques. You can either perform the activity with an instructor or use a recording. Do not expect your mind to remain calm. It will be restless, easily distracted, and busy. Yes, you have chosen to meditate and focus on your mind. This does not mean you will suddenly experience a calm mind. You cannot expect to train your dog overnight.

As mentioned earlier, meditation is an easy and straightforward process. You only need to practice it regularly. The only thing you need to do is close your eyes and focus on your breathing. Allow your mind to do what it wants. Meditation is the only skill where you do not have to achieve an objective. This activity is only a place where you do not have to put any effort.

Meditation is not good or bad. You are either aware or unaware. When you find yourself lost in thought and learn to reel yourself in, you become aware. This is when you learn to return to your object of focus—that is, your breath. You need to keep doing this if you want to return to your meditation process. Your objective should be to hone your awareness. When you persevere and meditate regularly, the period between your distraction and awareness will grow longer.

Before you start, you need to familiarize yourself with how your mind functions and works. You need to know what to expect when you begin to meditate. It is important to note that meditation does not solve any of your problems. You cannot expect a life filled with happiness simply because you meditate. Life will continue to happen, and it will throw different situations and uncertainties at you. Meditation helps you choose how you react to different situations. You will change the way you react. You also learn how to view a circumstance differently. When you practice consistently, you can change the way you feel about any situation. You become more aware and understand different aspects of life better.

The Practicalities

Before you look at how meditation helps in Tai Chi, you will first learn about the different practicalities you need to remember.

Find the Right Place and Time

The objective is to commit to meditating regularly. You need to meditate at least a few times each week if possible. You must be clear about how much time you want to spend on meditation. You also need to determine where you want to sit. Since this is a habit you need to develop, it will take perseverance and discipline. It is only when you honor the routine that you can build on your practice. Most people meditate around the same time, just like they perform a routine habit, such as brushing their teeth or eating breakfast. This is the only way they can remember to meditate. It is best to meditate every morning. Alternatively, you can find a time that works for you.

Clothing

You can wear anything you want. The objective of meditation is to help you remain relaxed and comfortable. If you are wearing a belt, scarf, or tie, remove them before you sit down to meditate. Remove any uncomfortable clothing or tight shoes. You can also sit without any clothing in the comfort of your home if this helps you.

Position

Where you meditate and how you sit does not matter. You can either meditate outside or inside. You can choose to sit on a cushion, the floor, chair, bench, or any other place that works best for you. You can choose to sit in a cross-legged position under a tree if you want to follow the stereotypical images. If you are a beginner, you can sit in an upright position on a chair or the floor. You need to familiarize yourself with the practice. It is best to sit toward the front of the chair since that helps you keep your neck relaxed, your back straight, and your chin tucked in. Leave your hands on your lap.

Time

The time you spend meditating depends on your circumstances, the time available, and your preference. It is important to note that the time you spend on meditation is not as important as how often you meditate. When you begin with meditation, it is best to start with a short session. You can increase the time slowly until you become familiar with training your mind. If you cannot sit in silence for a long time, you can choose a three-minute session. Give meditation a shot and learn to improve your skills as your confidence grows.

Define Your Motivation

People meditate for different reasons, and for this reason, nobody can define the reasons. It is always helpful for you to start with a clear idea about why you want to meditate. If you do not have a clear motivation in mind, you cannot meditate. You will struggle to maintain this habit. When you are clear about your motivation, you know exactly what you want from the session. You may choose to meditate to be more focused, feel calmer, and be less stressed or be happier. This motivation will help you maintain the right attitude. You also learn to commit and maintain the practice of meditation.

Take Each Day as it Comes

Bear in mind that meditation is a practice. You cannot expect to sprint and learn everything in one session. You cannot expect instant progress. Take every session as it comes. You need to appreciate the skill and commit to it. Be patient and practice regularly. You will feel the benefits of this practice over time. Meditation is neither good nor bad, and you cannot succeed or fail. Meditation only focuses on non-awareness and awareness. Through meditation, you learn to let go of distractions. The more your mind learns about your thoughts and emotions, the more you learn to become aware. You learn to eliminate distractions.

Learn to Stay Mindful After Meditation

When you meditate, you learn to practice being in the present moment. You learn to be more aware of what is happening now. The objective of meditation is to remove any distractions during the day and become more mindful of your thoughts. When you finish your session, take time to recognize how your thoughts have changed. You need to intend to carry on this feeling throughout your day. You also need to develop a clear idea of what you will do immediately after your meditation session. This can be any activity. You can jump off the seat and become active straight away. Try not to let go of the spacious quality you developed during the meditation session, so be more aware of this quality regardless of the type of activity you perform.

Use Body Scans

One of the best ways to begin with meditation if you are a beginner is through a body scan. This technique is one of the easiest ways to cultivate the curiosity you need to bring to meditation. So, what is a body scan? Consider a photocopier or X-ray machine. This machine is slowly moving on every part of your body. It detects the different physical sensations in your body and any changes you may make in your body. This machine does not analyze any of your thoughts or change the way you feel.

This book will now explain the technique a little better. You close your eyes and start focusing on the top of your head. You need to scan your body from your head to your toes mentally. As you perform this scan, notice the parts of your body that are tensed and those that are relaxed. Identify the parts of your body that are uncomfortable or comfortable. The only thing you are doing is developing a picture of how your body feels. Take twenty seconds to complete this process. You may find yourself distracted and different thoughts may arise. If you are distracted, go back to the part of your body where you left off. When you make this technique a part of your practice, you become familiar with your feelings and emotions.

Obstacles Beginners Often Face

If you are a beginner and meditating for the first time, you will encounter a few obstacles. You may be bored, anxious, overwhelmed, generally resistant, restless, or worried. When you continue to meditate, you learn to overcome these obstacles. The process becomes easier. It is important to remember that you approach meditation only with a lifetime of being conditioned. Your mind is always busy, and it cannot work with stillness. So, your mind will not work in your favor until it adjusts to the idea of not doing anything and letting things go.

Finding the Time

Most people face a common obstacle when it comes to meditation: They cannot find the time to meditate. It is important to note that you can miss meditation for a few days a week. It is important to practice meditation regularly, but if you can pick up from your last session and learn to give yourself time to meditate, you learn to improve the health of your mind. If you last meditated a week or month ago, revisit the basics because your mind may not remember everything you taught it.

Feeling Drowsy

It is normal for people to fall asleep or feel drowsy when they meditate. If you are a beginner, this can happen frequently. The mind believes that doing nothing means you are relaxing. You will learn to differentiate between total relaxation, which results from meditation, and relaxed focus, which you achieve through meditation. The following are a few tips you can use to remain alert and awake:

• Do not lie down when you meditate. Maintain an upright posture.

- It is best to meditate in the morning when your mind is a little brighter and you are not tired after your day at work or school.
- Let fresh air into the room.

Multiple Distractions

Most beginners believe you need complete silence when you meditate. If you have this thought in mind, any distraction or sound around you will make you extra sensitive. However, you do not have to sit in complete silence when you meditate. You need to settle down in your environment and let the sounds surrounding you become background noise. Children are going to yell in the street, and your neighbors may play loud music. Learn to settle into your background. Do not dwell on the sounds around you. Try to tune the sounds out and avoid getting frustrated. If you are a beginner, you will struggle with this, but you can use noise-canceling earphones or earplugs to help you during your session.

Stereotypes

Meditation is a practice or tradition that comes with numerous stigmas and misconceptions attached to it. Meditation is a practice built on the back of many stereotypes built on the back of various media, rumors, and myths. Most people associate meditation with different images and labels they may have read or seen. Bear in mind that you do not need a "specific" personality to meditate. Anybody can meditate. People who want to understand their minds better can start meditating—so can you.

One of the biggest misconceptions or myths of meditation is that it is a religious practice. You need to understand that meditation does not rely on your belief system, but it is a skill. Some people meditate in certain religions; however, using this skill in religious practices does not make meditating religious.

Another stereotype is that people believe meditation is serious. You need to sit in a cross-legged position, extend your arms, and repeat a sound loudly. The truth is very different. You can choose to sit in a cross-legged position, by the beach, in nature, or even meditate on a chair. The only thing you need to do is become aware of everything that happens in your mind. You need to focus on your feelings and emotions. Since everyone has different thoughts, they struggle differently. Many athletes have begun to use meditation to help them calm their minds. They use this to train their minds to not get in their way when they participate.

People who meditate do not hug trees or burn incense when they meditate. There is nothing wrong with doing either of these things. The only thing people do when they meditate is get inside their minds and start to understand their thinking processes.

Learn to Stick with the Routine

You can start something new easily, whether it is an exercise regime, a hobby, or a diet. The hard part is to continue performing this activity. Your enthusiasm will begin to wane, and the novelty of the new activity will wear off. This is something that happens with meditation, too. Since the exercises are repetitive, you may get bored. It is important to remember that you are training your mind to work the way you relate to your feelings and thoughts. It will take time, discipline, and perseverance to manage your thoughts and emotions.

People stop meditating because their minds will not allow them to find peace. It is also important to note that your mind is constantly going to think. Your mind is programmed to behave this way. Through meditation, you cannot expect your thoughts to stop completely. Meditation only teaches you how to step back and observe each thought carefully without any bias or judgment. The objective of meditation is to let your thoughts pass through your mind freely. This is a skill you need to master, learn, and practice. You can only do this if you learn to build the habit.

It is only when you stick to your practice of meditation that you will reap its benefits. When you feel the benefits, you learn to understand how your mind feels and thinks. You also learn to take a step toward a happier and healthier life with increased contentment, compassion, calm, and clarity.

Several people refer to Tai Chi as moving meditation. Since this martial art uses graceful and slow movements, it can be used as a meditation technique. This technique helps you maintain focus and control your thoughts and emotions. Tai Chi meditation also leaves you with a feeling of relaxation, which helps you release any inner tensions.

Tai Chi and Meditation

Tai Chi focuses on the flow of energy throughout your body. This science is termed neigong. Every Taoist energy or Qigong system in China uses this science as its foundation. Most martial arts use some or all of the information and techniques that derive from this science. Neigong is the root of the work of chi and is used in martial arts, such as Hsing-I, Bagua and Tai Chi, Chinese medicine techniques, and Taoist meditation. This science is also used in bodywork systems. If you want to learn Tai Chi or any other form of these martial arts, you need to start with the basic movements.

For instance, there are long and short Tai Chi forms, and you have looked at these in detail in the third chapter of the book. Bagua, on the other hand, uses a single palm change or circle walking change. The different components of neigong, over time, will allow you to incorporate the movements and manage the energy easily. You can do this by opening different channels of energy in your body, spirit, and mind.

It is important to learn and understand the components that are relevant to practicing and manipulating energy. You may only learn the basics when you start by practicing this art. As you continue to work, you will move on and learn deeper aspects of the art. You can only do this if you are willing to incorporate the movements to understand your thoughts and emotions. You will constantly return to the different neigong components in the art to learn more about the different powerful and refined applications and aspects within these movements.

There are sixteen components you need to learn, and the sequence is not set in stone. Many people find it easier to learn more about the alignment and breathing components before moving on to find a way to relax and heal. If you are a Tai Chi practitioner, you will experience systematic and progressive physical and mental health improvements. You also learn more about the spiritual and energetic capabilities of your spirit, mind, and body. This combination of different techniques is what makes Tai Chi and other martial arts great for spiritual practices.

Finding Emptiness

When it comes to Taoism or Taoist traditions, you need to embark on a spiritual path that goes beyond having a calm, peaceful, and healthy mind. The objective of Taoist meditation is to make sure that you become aware of the unchanging and permanent center of your existence. You need to find the place of emptiness and spirit. This is your consciousness. Taoist meditation is a way to relax your mind and soul. You need to relax your very being or soul.

Tai Chi is an art that helps you deepen your understanding of your thoughts, awareness, and the ability to relax on every level. The objective of Tai Chi and the practice of the art is an advanced form of Taoist meditation. You explore different opposites and learn the essence of non-duality and emptiness. These concepts are the foundation of Wu Chi and Tai Chi. You can practice these methods by altering the rhythms of the yin and yang. You only need to perform the movements slowly.

The objective of Tai Chi or moving meditation is difficult to recognize. You need to find the place in your mind where you can combine these differentiations and unite with the emptiness in your mind and soul.

Tai Chi Meditation Techniques

Now, look at a few meditation techniques used in Tai Chi.

Standing Meditation

Cynthia McMullen is an LMT from the Oriental Healing Arts of Massage Therapy, Traditional Taoist Medical Qigong, and Acupuncture in Arizona. She states that meditation is extremely important when performing Tai Chi since it centers and grounds you emotionally and physically. You learn to identify stillness and calm within movements. Since Tai Chi uses standing movements, you use standing meditation when you perform any movement. Follow the steps given below if you want to master this form of meditation.

- You need to stand in a comfortable position. Make sure your feet are shoulder-width apart and your toes are pointing ahead. You can keep your knees relaxed if you want to.

- Tuck your hips a little forward and bend your shoulders downward and keep them relaxed.

- Now, lift your head and hold it high. Do not put too much stress on your neck.

- Take a deep breath and exhale slowly through your nostrils. Now, close your eyes and start focusing on each breath you take. You can keep your eyes slightly open if you want to.

- Focus only on your connection to the ground. Pay attention to your feet and how they feel on the surface of the earth.

- When you inhale, visualize that the energy from the surface around you or the earth is the energy being pulled into your feet.

When you exhale, release the energy from your body and let it return to the source.

Continue to perform this exercise fifteen times. Let the energy travel from your legs to the rest of your body. The energy should reach the center of your being. The center of your being is at the sacral chakra, which is right below your belly button. When you exhale, visualize that all the unclean and toxic energy from your body is leaving.

Variations

McMullen also mentioned there are variations to the standing technique. Several variations include arms around the shoulders, seated meditation, meditation with the feet wider than shoulder-width apart, etc.

Focus on Breathing

Dr. Paul Lam is from the Tai Chi Association in Australia. He mentioned that breathing techniques are important when it comes to Tai Chi meditation. When you perform Tai Chi, you need to focus on the energy moving between your body and the surrounding area. It is important to note that Tai Chi focuses on the giving and taking of energy. The foundation of this form of meditation is extremely easy. You only need to think of absorbing energy when you inhale and releasing it when you exhale. Most Tai Chi movements and meditations use this technique.

Open and Close Movements

Lam also mentioned that you could use open and closed movements when you want to meditate. When you perform opening movements, you need to place your hands in front of your chest. As you inhale, you need to open your arms, step forward, and open them wide open. When you exhale, move your hands closer together and let go of all the pent-up energy. Lam also mentioned that you could apply the same rules when you move up and down. When you move your hands upward, you need to take a deep breath in. As you exhale, get rid of all the toxic energy and let go. When you stand up and bend down, you should breathe in and exhale, respectively.

Tai Chi and Breathing

You may be overwhelmed with the details and other information about Tai Chi. This is another topic that may overwhelm you if you are a beginner. However, you do not have to worry too much about Tai Chi breathing. The objective should be to learn how to move when you practice Tai Chi. Your breathing will improve when you perform and practice Tai Chi. When you learn the form completely and have practiced for a while, you need to learn how to breathe. You will also learn when to inhale and exhale.

Common postures used in Tai Chi are waving, windmills, and whips. The practice of these movements is more about the placement of the various parts of your body. Your breathing is of utmost importance because your breath is what guides you. Ramel Rones, a Tai Chi master, states, "When practiced regularly, Tai Chi can lead to better health and a higher quality of physical and emotional life." Regardless of whether you perform Tai Chi movements or any other workout, you need to breathe effectively to make sure you meet your fitness goals.

Tai Chi breathing is like the high any runner or athlete will achieve when exercise does not leave them feeling exhausted. This form of breathing will help calm your body down to achieve the balance to perform the exercise in a flow. When you find yourself in this position, you can start working on improving your movements.

If you want to find yourself in that zone, you need to focus on the lower energy center in your body. This center is in the sacral chakra, which is right below your belly button. You need to learn to tap into this area when you perform Tai Chi. This is the only way you can improve your movements and release any stress. Experts recommend that you visualize yourself inhaling and exhaling the energy in this chakra when performing any movement.

Performing Tai Chi Breathing

Follow the steps given below if you want to perform Tai Chi breathing:

- You can either sit or stand in a comfortable position. Let your hand rest on your lap or lower abdomen. If you want to perform Tai Chi breathing, you need to let your tongue rest on the roof of your mouth. You also need to breathe only through your nose. If you want to use Tai Chi breathing when you perform the exercise, it is best to leave this passageway open. You can use both your mouth and nose to breathe when you perform these movements. As you practice, you will learn to breathe only through your nose.

- Take a deep breath and use your diaphragm to push the air into your lungs. Focus on your hands when you inhale. You will see that your hands move upward when you inhale and fall when you exhale.

- You should let your breathing be continuous. When one breath ends, you need to move to the next. Every inhalation and exhalation should form a loop. There should be no end. The objective is to achieve the meditative state where breathing comes naturally to you. Your breathing should be effortless.

- You should now relax your body and let your breath become deeper and longer.

Why You Shouldn't Focus on Tai Chi Breathing

Every movement performed in Tai Chi is scripted. This means the movements are frequently corrected. Most people naturally believe there is breathwork that corresponds to each movement you make. If you focus too much on your breath, you will forget why you want to perform Tai Chi. The objective is only to return and relax the body so you find balance and equilibrium.

It is also hard to define what Tai Chi breathing is all about since different forms of Tai Chi use different breathing patterns. You need to make sure you maintain long continuous breaths. Several movements in Tai Chi also require you to take quick, short breaths. You can employ these breaths when you perform long movements or want to transition quickly from one movement to the next.

When you use standard instructions for breathing when you perform different Tai Chi movements, you do not focus on your current energy state. You also forget about the energy you began with. Assume you enter work or class hyper because you drank too much coffee. When you go back home, perhaps you are exhausted or under the weather because of the work you did. How you start the movements and breaths at the start of any form is different from when you end that form.

The most important thing to remember is that people have different levels of coordination, speed of movements, and lung capacities. If you try to match anybody else, you may only hamper your progress. The subsequent sections will discuss how breathing affects your Tai Chi movements. Different Tai Chi breathing exercises allow you to isolate the breathing from the movement you make.

Now that you have an idea of what Tai Chi breathing is look at a few tips to help you reap the benefits of Tai Chi breathing.

Guidelines for Tai Chi Breathing

Yes, there are no rules for how you should breathe when you perform Tai Chi. This does not mean you can breathe any way you want to. You need to adhere to the following guidelines when you perform Tai Chi:

• When you exhale, breathe out slowly. Exhale for as long as you can. This will leave you feeling like you need to inhale deeply.

• You need to exhale for longer than you inhale.

• Let your tongue stick to the roof of your mouth. If you do not know where to place it, say "la" and see where your tongue is. You need to leave the tongue in this position when you practice Tai Chi.

• Inhale and exhale only through your nose. Do not use your mouth unless you suffer from a cold or an allergy that causes nasal congestion.

• Aim for continuous and long breaths. Do not pause between inhalation and exhalation. Do not stop breathing.

• You must inhale into your belly. When you breathe, the pressure on your organs will change, and each breath massages the organs.

• As you inhale, your body will store energy. So, as you inhale, think of oxygen entering your body. When you deliver this force or energy, you can exhale slowly.

• When you move your hands apart, you need to breathe in deeply. This means you are storing energy.

• If you move your hands up, you need to take a deep breath and store the energy. When you move your hands down, exhale and release the energy into the universe.

Integrating Tai Chi Breathing into Your Workout

According to several classical and ancient Tai Chi texts and documents, you can overcome weight problems with less physical effort using Tai Chi. This suggests that Tai Chi is a better way to complete a workout since it is less stressful on your body. Rones stated, "Through correct postural alignment, deep breathing, an empty mind, and grounding or rooting [connecting with the earth beneath your feet], one can reach a state of effortless action."

The following tips can help you focus on Tai Chi breathing when you perform the movements.

Observe Your Breath

Before you learn to adjust your breathing to follow Tai Chi breathing, you need to become aware of how you currently breathe. You may assume your body only inhales and exhales when you need air, but it will react differently under stress. You may breathe sporadically or in short bursts under stress. When you become mindful about your breath, you can correct any irregularities with ease. You will only need to focus on deep, slow breaths.

Count it Out

If you find yourself unable to breathe, inhale for three seconds and exhale for five seconds. Count every breath you take. The objective is to breathe in a way that feels natural. Do not force your breath. When you gasp for air while you work out, it means you are pushing your limits too hard. Learn to focus on your breathing in such situations. Draw deliberate and deep breaths. Use your diaphragm to take deeper breaths. Check your progress every few minutes to make sure you breathe easily and efficiently. This is the only way you can improve your performance and movements.

Pace Yourself

If you do not want to follow the three- and five-second breaths mentioned in the previous section, you can switch to a shorter duration. You can inhale for one second and exhale for two seconds. You can reduce the speed at which you perform the movements in Tai Chi if you feel tired quickly. If you think it is too fast, take a little more time to breathe in and out. When you perform any strenuous movements, you need to inhale and exhale to make sure your breathing guides your movements. For instance, when you need to bend your knees and move your arms at the same time, inhale when you lower your body and exhale when you move your arms to either side.

Be Self-Aware in Your Routine

It is important to pay attention to what your body is saying to you. You can work out and perform strenuous movements on one day, while you may not have the energy to do this on the next day. So, become aware of how you feel, both physically and mentally. When you practice this, you become more sensitive to what your body has to say. You become more aware, and your performance improves. If you want to do this, you need to ask yourself the following questions when you perform Tai Chi:

- Do I enjoy Tai Chi?
- Is there a way I can enhance the effect the workout has on me?
- Is my breathing too fast?
- Am I connected to my body?

Relax

According to your brain, you need to breathe if you want to live. So, when you stop breathing in, your mind will switch into the fight-or-flight mode. This will lead to panicked and short breaths to make up for the lack of oxygen in your body. If you want to prevent this from happening, you need to slow down and take a few deep breaths. Start observing your breath.

When you practice these steps, your breathing style will improve. If you need an energy booster to go faster, longer, and further, you need to learn how to tap into the energy stored in your body. It is only easy to do this when you maintain your breath.

Why You Shouldn't Pay Too Much Attention to Breathing

If you only focus on your breathing, it can lead to the following consequences:

- If you hold your breath for too long, it can cause anxiety. This will only cause stress, and it defies the purpose of Tai Chi.

- When you relax, the energy from your body moves to your feet or dantian. If you use too much pressure, which you use in Qigong breathing, you may push the energy in the wrong direction.

- You can only feel the energy in your body moving from one organ to the next if you let your breath move freely. You need to learn how to sense your breath and feel it before you manipulate it.

- The worst-case scenario is intestinal problems. If you are under too much pressure, your hemorrhoids can flare up, and you may develop intestinal issues.

The objective of Tai Chi is always to focus on the present and your center. You need to find a balance between your mind, body, and spirit. You can do this easily through Tai Chi breathing. Most people who find themselves in a state, such as being stressed, tired, or agitated, will feel happy and calm after performing Tai Chi breathing. This is something powerful.

Chapter Six: Stances and Footwork

Tai Chi Stances

Before you look at the different training techniques you need to follow in Tai Chi, you will learn about the most important aspect: the fundamental stances. It is only when you perform these stances that you develop a strong foundation of the various postures you need to use when you perform different Tai Chi movements.

You can understand the set of exercises well when you understand these stances. If you are a beginner, you will need to perform these stances and master them if you want to strengthen your muscles. Practice these stances if you want to use your mind to help you practice the different Tai Chi stances. These movements help you coordinate between your movements, breathing, and mind.

When you learn the basics of training, you need to move toward Qigong. Moving Qigong will help you feel the movements the way you need to. The movements will help you maintain and harmonize the energy in your mind, spirit, and body. You can also manage your chi. This book will discuss a few other stances and movements later. Like other martial arts forms, Tai Chi has its fundamental stances, and these are the basics for movement, stability, and martial art techniques. There are eight important stances in Tai Chi, and none of these stances use any hand sequence.

In this chapter, you will look at eight stances. You can ignore the position of your hands when you perform these stances.

Ma Bu or Horse Stance

This stance is often used when you move from one movement to the next. You can use this even when you move from one technique to the next. If you want to perform this stance, you need to perform the steps given below:

- Place your feet wider than shoulder-width apart.
- Bend the knees slowly until the angle between your calves and rear thighs is almost 90 degrees.
- Keep your back straight.
- Relax yourself and center your thoughts and emotions.
- Your knees should be in line with your toes and your feet flat on the ground.

If you want to reduce the stress placed on your body, keep your feet relaxed. This reduces the risk of injury. Your knees should always be in line with your toes when you perform this stance.

Gong JianBu, Deng Shan Bu, Bow-Arrow Stance or Mountain Climbing Stance

This is an important stance since it is an offensive stance used in Tai Chi. To perform this stance, you need to follow the steps given below:

- Place one leg in front of the other. Your toes and knees should be perpendicular to the ground.
- The front leg should support at least 60 percent of your weight.

- The toe of the leg, which is in the lead position, should point toward the inside at a 15-degree angle.

- Set the rear leg firmly on the ground until it supports your body's weight. You can bend the rear leg a little in this stance.

- Maintain the upper body at a 90-degree angle from the ground.

If you make a mistake when it comes to maintaining this stance, you may hurt your knee.

Zuo Pan Bu or Sitting on Crossed Legs Stance

This is a forward movement. You need to first switch to the first stance, the ma bu stance. Once you do this, you need to turn the right foot and body in a clockwise direction. You need to maintain a 90-degree angle between the right foot while you pivot or move on the left foot. You can do the same on your left side. Try to hold the position for at least one minute if you are a beginner. If you have practiced this stance, you can maintain it for at least five minutes.

Si Liu Bu or Four-Six Stance

This stance is used when you try to defend yourself. When it comes to weight distribution, this stance is the opposite of the second stance you looked at. The front leg should support at least forty percent of your weight. Shift the remaining weight onto the back leg. Your rear leg should be slightly bent, and the toes and knees should be turned toward the inside. Hold the front leg slightly loose and bend it. Do not strain any part of your body.

Fu Hu Bu or Tame the Tiger Stance

The tame the tiger stance is used for defense. You can also use this stance when you perform low attacks. Follow the steps given below to assume this stance:

- Stand with your feet shoulder-width apart.

- While keeping one leg straight, lower your body slowly while squatting down on one leg.

- When you squat, your thigh should be parallel to the floor.
- Your feet need to be flat on the ground, while the knee of the squatting leg is in line with your toes.

Xu Bu, Xuan Ji Bu or False Stance

The false stance helps to strengthen your body to increase the intensity of your kicks. To perform this stance, follow the steps given below:

- Stand with your feet together and shift your weight onto one leg.
- Now, set the other leg in front of your body.
- Your foot should not be on the ground. Your toes should only hover slightly above the ground.
- Now use the leg to kick.

Jin Gi Du Li or Golden Rooster Stance

This stance is one legged and will take you time to perfect. This stance is like the previous stance and serves the same purpose. This stance increases the strength in your legs, thereby making it easier for you to perform kicks. Follow the steps given below to perform this stance:

- Stand with your feet shoulder-width apart.
- Slowly lift your knee. Your toes should point downward at a 45-degree angle.
- Now kick using this leg.

Zuo Dun or Squat Stance

This stance is used when you need to work on your knees. When you perform this stance, you train your knees. To perform this stance, follow the steps given below:

Place Your Feet Shoulder-Width Apart

Lower your body slowly until your knees are at ninety degrees. Your thighs should be parallel to the floor. Keep your back straight.

Try to stay in this position for at least one minute if you are a beginner. Focus on keeping your mind calm when you perform this stance. If you have mastered the stance, you can stay in this position for longer than five minutes. Do not stress your body too much; just start slowly.

Fundamental Footwork

If you have watched someone performing Tai Chi, you will be struck by how beautifully the person performs the art. There is an economy, clarity, control, and grace in every move they make. Many factors come into play when mastering Tai Chi and the different movements in the art. Having said that, when you master fundamental footwork, you can find control and balance. This is fundamental when it comes to Tai Chi. To master Tai Chi, you need to master a few specific movements.

Since Tai Chi has its roots in martial arts, much emphasis is placed on your readiness to react. It is important for you to control and maintain your movements. You need to shift the weight easily from one side of your body to the other with ease while keeping your back straight. These movements are essential if you want to be responsive and maintain balance and stability.

Now compare this to your regular movements. When you walk, you move forward. Your body weight is maintained between the legs. You put one leg in front of the other to avoid falling. When you push a trolley toward the airport's baggage claim, you push your body weight into the trolley to make it move or continue the motion.

The knowledge or understanding your body has about how you should move is very different from the movements you use in Tai Chi. If you want to master Tai Chi, you need to understand how your body should move based on the Tai Chi principles. Since you make subconscious movements in Tai Chi, you are often unaware of whether you conform to the principles. If you are a beginner, this is going to be difficult. There are many things you need to master when it comes to Tai Chi, including:

- The shape of every movement and transition.
- The position of the feet and hands.
- The coordination of the lower and upper body.

You can only focus on the footwork once you are comfortable with the stances and the basic form for Tai Chi. The following are the most important facts to bear in mind when it comes to your footwork:

- You need to move your weight off one foot when you lift your leg.
- Place your foot in front of you before you shift your weight onto it.
- Transfer your weight using your legs.

These points might seem obvious to you, and it is easy to improve if you make an effort.

Shifting Your Weight Off the Foot Before Lifting It

Most daily activities require you to center your weight. It becomes easy to forget about shifting your weight when you move your feet. When you perform a set of Tai Chi exercises, you try to support your weight on one leg only. If you want to maintain control and balance, you need to shift your weight to the supporting leg. Do not place any additional weight on the foot you are about to lift.

Shifting the Weight After Placing Your Foot on the Ground

Martial arts influences this area of footwork. If you perform Tai Chi on slippery or uneven ground, you need to commit and control your weight; otherwise, you will lose balance. If you are not focused and committed to the movement, you need to adjust your stance. If you do not place your foot firmly on the ground before you push any weight onto it, you may experience the following:

- Slamming your foot into the ground when you land.
- Leaning forward while holding the position.
- Maintaining a wider or longer stance that is not comfortable for you.
- Inability to balance.

When you work on maintaining your weight and controlling how you place the weight on your foot, you naturally take shorter steps. You also find yourself in control when you enter or leave a stance. Kicks are the best way to check if you can control the movement of the weight. Once you master the art of landing, you can shift your weight forward. This makes it easier for you to move into the new stance or movement. It is important to maintain your weight when you transition between different movements. You need to check yourself when you move into simpler movements to ensure you are shifting your weight correctly. If you do not focus on your balance when you perform simple stances, you will find it difficult to manage your weight when you move onto harder sets.

Shifting the Weight Using Your Legs

Assume you use a typist chair to support your torso. The chair has wheels at the bottom and moves forward and backward easily. It also comes with a central pole that allows you to shift your body from side to side. When you shift your weight forward, you only need to use your legs. You should avoid using your torso. The leg placed to the front should be relaxed. This means there should be no weight placed on that leg. You should use your back leg to give you the push needed to move the chair forward.

If you use this image, you know you can manage your height level easily. When you perform this movement, you use the muscles in your legs more. This movement tires the muscles in your legs if you perform it correctly. You learn to use your legs more when you perform these functions. You no longer lean your torso forward when you perform this movement.

Once you master these characteristics, you can perform economic, smooth, clean, and clear movements. Make a conscious effort to perform these movements to ensure you do not go back to your previous footwork.

Remember that the classic texts state, "*The energy is routed in the feet, develops in the legs, is directed by the waist, and moves up to the fingers. The feet, legs, and waist must act as one so that when advancing and retreating, you will obtain a good opportunity and a superior position... If you fail to gain these advantages, your body will be in a state of disorder and confusion. The only way to correct this fault is by adjusting your legs and waist.*"

Chapter Seven: Hand Movements

Tai Chi is a form of martial arts, both at the lowest and highest levels. You need to adhere to every movement you make and abide by all martial arts principles. Most people make the mistake of looking at Tai Chi as a meditation art. It is important to remember that Tai Chi is a form of martial arts, and you need to study it in this way.

Now that you have this in mind, you will next learn how you can use your hands when you perform Tai Chi. Your hands are your main tools when you interact with your surrounding environment. Your hands hold more than one-quarter of the bones in your body, and around one-fifth of your muscles are used to perform hand movements. When you perform a gesture using your hand, you use at least fifty muscles. There are close to 21,000 sensors of pressure, pain, and heat. You can destroy, heal, and cause pain or pleasure using your hand.

Every tool is designed to perform different tasks. When you use a hammer to sink a nail into a piece of wood, you know it can complete this task. Your hands are designed to do the same as well. They are designed to perform specific movements. Your slender and long fingers can be used to grasp your opponent's hands or fingers. Every part of your hand has been designed for specific functions like tools. You can get the job done in different ways to safeguard yourself.

Bear in mind that you can use your human hand to create different designs. Your hands are limited to a few specific and general tasks, but they have evolved to be used in numerous ways. When you perform Tai Chi, your hands can be used in different ways. You can use variations of these movements to the best of your abilities. You can twist, push, pull, grab, chop, poke, smash, neutralize, slap, strike, adhere, and perform many other movements. Your hands can perform different movements at the same time. You cannot slap your opponent with one finger or grab something with a fist in the same way you cannot cut wood using a hammer. You can use your finger to poke and your fist to punch.

Most Tai Chi practitioners avoid changing their hand postures before they perform different hand movements during their practice. This is a shortcoming since you need to understand how to change hand postures to maintain form. When you change postures, you are letting your body know your intent. Your intent is what drives your practice, and this intent will help you succeed.

The next few sections look at some basic hand positions, their use, and how you can express each of these movements in Tai Chi.

Hand Postures

Normal Hand

This is the simplest and most common hand position used by every Tai Chi practitioner. You maintain this movement when you do not want to perform any movements. This hand is aware of the energy in it. In most martial arts, which use an open hand technique, this hand is called the "at ready" hand. When you hold your hands in a normal position while you wait to do something, it is just relaxing. Most people use this movement to transition between different hand movements. Some examples of where this hand movement is used are the waiting hand used in the Repulse Monkey position or the Fist Under the Elbow.

Tiger's Mouth

This hand movement is used while performing offense moves, including twisting, grabbing, pulling, and neutralizing. The hand movement is open, and there is a lot of space between your index finger and thumb. This movement gives you the ability to clasp and grasp anything between your fingers and thumb. This is an active posture that allows you to twist and grab onto your opponent's arms easily. It is best you do not use this movement when you strike your opponent because it does not do well for strikes. The energy in your palm will be dissipated if you use the movement in a large area. Since your thumb sticks out, your opponent can choose to attack it. Some examples of the use of this movement include the hand used in the High Pat on a Horse, the hand used in the Brush Knee, and the Pulling Hand used in other movements.

Striking Palm

When you perform this hand gesture, hold your thumb close to your palm. Your fingers should be held back slightly and need to be erect. The energy in your palm should be maintained in the lower end of the palm. The bones in the forearm are close to the surface, and you need to protect them from harm. This movement allows you to use the energy found in the palm and project it into your opponent's body. Some examples of this hand movement include Repulse Monkey, Fan Through the Back, and Brush Knee.

Neutralizing and Pushing Hand

This hand movement is used often to either neutralize or push your hand. This is the step between the Tiger's Mouth and relaxed hand movements. You can mold this hand movement in your favor to ensure the movement is soft. This movement allows you to attach the hand to a surface and transmit energy. You need to hold the thumb close to the palm if you want to use the Tiger's Mouth. If you want to use the Striking Palm movement, you need to spread your fingers out slightly. Some examples of this movement include the Withdraw and Push movement, the Push movement, Roll Back and Brush Knee.

Slapping Palm

For this hand movement, you need to keep your hand open. Do not place your thumb on your palm, but only close to it. This hand movement is softer when compared to other hand movements. You can use it to whip your opponent. The objective of this hand movement is not to let the energy penetrate easily. You want to retain your energy. Tai Chi experts often use this movement to confuse their opponents while preparing for other movements. One example of this movement is the High Pat on a Horse, which is discussed in the next section.

Chopping Hand

In this hand movement, you need to hold your fingers firmly together. This motion uses peng energy. Tuck the thumb into your palm, and ensure the energy is focused on the edge of your hand. You can use this energy to chop or move the hand in a downward and upward motion. Some examples of this movement include the upward chop used in the Slanting Flying and the downward chop used in the Deflect Downward movement.

Finger Poke Hand

In this movement, you need to maintain a firm hold. Hold your fingers straight and tuck the thumb into your palm. Your palm, fingers, wrist, and forearm must be in a straight line. When you poke your opponent using this movement, you place excess stress on the joints that are not maintained in a straight line. Some examples of this movement include White Snake Pulls Tongue Out, Needle at the Bottom of the Sea, and Cross Hands.

Striking Using the Back of the Hand

This hand movement is extremely difficult to perform. You need to find a way to master it since the energy used is limited as the bones present in the back of your hand are close to the surface. You may damage or break them easily if you do not use them correctly. You need to use this motion if you want to distract or stun anybody and so, often, your aim will be the person's nose. Fold your fingers to form a ball to ensure the energy is stored in the knuckle area of your hand. One example of this movement is the White Snake.

Fist

You can use the fist in different ways when you perform Tai Chi. You can chop, punch, and use the side, front, or back of your hand. If you use your knuckles, you can use them to protrude or focus energy on your opponent's small areas. One of the most common fist movements used is the straight punch. To perform this movement, you need to close your fist. Do not close it too tightly.

When you punch an opponent, you need to focus on the index and middle fingers. It is only because of the strength in those knuckles that you can throw the strongest punch. Keep your wrist, hand, and forearm in one line to ensure the force only comes from the back of the hand. You need to ensure you do not use your arm badly so that you do not hurt yourself. If your arm is bent at the wrong angle, you do not release all the force in your arm.

You need to use the half twist movement when you perform a punch in Tai Chi. Using this movement allows you to end the motion using your thumb. Keep your palm facing upward and then concentrate and focus on the energy. Do not use a full twist since that will only leave you punching your opponent with your fist facing downward. This will put too much pressure or stress on the tissues connecting your elbow, wrist, and shoulder.

Hook Hand

When you perform the single whip movement, you can use this hand movement. This is a great tool to strike your opponent on the sides. You can also use it to strike them in the wrist area, back of the hand, and knuckles. The hook hand movement can be used to poke your opponent. The movement allows you to focus your energy on small areas of your hand. It also allows you to neutralize the opponent by wrapping your fingers around their wrist. If you learn the yang style of Tai Chi, you will learn ten different types of single whips. You can perform a variation of this movement but try to integrate different hook hands and movements into a single whip.

Tai Chi Movements

The following are some common Tai Chi movements that use the hand movements mentioned above.

Step Back and Repulse Monkey

When you perform this movement, you use the right hand to perform the tiger's mouth and the left hand to strike your palm. This movement allows you to grab your opponent's wrist easily using your right hand. Since they are holding onto your wrist tightly, you need to withdraw your arm slowly until your opponent is close to you. This makes them vulnerable to your strike.

Plane Cross Hands

In this movement, you can use a neutralizing palm. Use the opposite arm as your neutralizing palm. Press your palm slightly downward and toward your opponent's ribs. Use your other arm to poke your opponent. Do not use the tiger's mouth movement if you want to avoid dissipating the energy in the jing.

Single Whip

You can use this movement in different scenarios. When you perform this movement, use the Tiger's Mouth hand gesture to grab your opponent's left wrist. It is best to do this using the opposite hand so that you can strike your opponent in the ribs with your left hand.

White Snake Pulling the Tongue Out

When your opponent is close, you can strike them or protect yourself using your left hand to perform the neutralizing movement. You can then strike your hand against their nose. Use the back of your hand to do this. It is best to strike your opponent on the bridge of their nose since you can cause immense pain without putting in too much effort.

Fan Through Your Back

When your opponent punches you, you can use the Tiger's Mouth movement to grab your opponent's hand. As you pull their hand, you will expose the chest or rib area. You can then strike your opponent with your hand. If you want, you can punch your opponent for better results.

Hitting a Tiger

This movement is interesting and is also known as the Blocking Punch. When you perform this movement, you need to block your opponent's hook punch with your opposite arm. For instance, if your opponent uses his right arm, you need to use your left arm to block the movement. When you block the hook punch, you should also use your right hand to punch your opponent's temple. It will take you some time to learn how to block punches, but once you master them, you will find the movement effective.

Once you finish blocking him, you need to make the next move. Punch your opponent with your right fist in his center. This punch is powerful since you put your entire weight in the punch and use a short range. Some experts use both arms to punch their opponent, but this only comes with practice.

High Pat on Horse

When you perform this movement, you will need to use the tiger's mouth hand gesture to neutralize the movement and slap your opponent's hand. Alternatively, you can use your neutralizing hand to block your opponent's next punch. A slap is quite effective since it adds a slight weight to your opponent's wrist. This will upset their balance and core.

Chapter Eight: Tai Chi Warm-Up Exercises

In this chapter, you will look at some warm-up exercises to perform before you practice Tai Chi.

Warm-Up Exercises

The first two steps discussed in this chapter will involve a warm-up and stretching exercise. You need to combine these with Tai Chi movements and practice them regularly if you want to improve your flexibility. These movements will help you tone your muscles.

Before you begin to perform these warm-up exercises and other movements, keep the following points in mind:

- Wear comfortable and loose clothing.
- Ensure your shoes are well-fitting and flat.
- Do not use new movements that cause you pain or discomfort.
- Move only within your comfort range. When you perform a movement for the first time, you need to stretch. Do not stretch your body too much. Start slowly and increase the range slowly.

- Stretch on both sides if you need to.
- Every movement should be performed smoothly and slowly.

You can also choose to do any of the following if you need to:

- Walk around for a few minutes and shake your legs and hands. You can clench and unclench your hands if you want to. This will loosen your joints and body and prepare your body for the movements and exercises you perform.

- You can massage your muscles if you want to. Rub your palms together to generate some energy or qi. Move your palms over your lower back, shoulders, ankles, feet, and legs. Continue to rub your arms together to generate the heat.

- Take a shower or a short walk before you begin your warm-up.

Stretching

Perform the exercises listed in this section at least three times before you begin your workout. There is no sequence you need to follow when it comes to stretching. The following are some points to bear in mind:

- If you cannot balance your body, you can use the wall or a chair to support you.
- Stretch only up to 60 percent of your normal range. You can increase the range slowly if you want to.

You will stretch the most important parts of your body before you perform the movements. You need to stretch your neck, spine, shoulders, knees, ankles, and hips. Since you will only perform two exercises for each part, you can remember them easily. It is important to remember that you will work from the top of your body to the bottom. Keep your feet shoulder-width apart when you perform these exercises unless it is otherwise specified.

Neck

Moving your head back

- Take a deep breath and move your hands up slowly above your head.
- Visualize that two balloons are lifting your wrists slowly.
- Turn your palms to face the wall in front of you. This makes sure your palms point upward.
- Bring your palms toward your chest and push your neck forward. Now, bend your chin backward.

Moving your head down

- Exhale and slowly outstretch your arms in front of you. Extend them fully.
- Now, press your hands down while making sure you do not bend your elbows.
- Slowly move your head toward your chest.

Turning your head

- Lift your right hand to your side and keep your palms facing upward.
- Turn your head to the right and look at the palm. Your left leg should be left at your hip, with your palm facing downward.
- Move your right hand to the right and turn your head while you focus on your palms.
- Now move your face back to the center.
- Perform the same steps with your other hand.

You can perform these exercises as many times as you want to. Release the muscles in your neck.

Shoulders

Rolling your shoulders

You need to roll your shoulders backward and forward to release the muscles. This makes it easier for you to perform movements easily.

Gathering energy

- Take a deep breath and lift your arms to the side. You can keep your elbows soft. Your palms should face upward. Now, move your arms until they curve over your head.
- When you exhale, you need to press your hands downward.
- Move your arms until they are below your belly button.

Spine

Stretching the spine

- Lift your hands in front of you and pretend you are carrying an exercise ball. Inhale deeply.
- Exhale deeply and push your hand upward. Visualize that you are pushing your hand against the wall or ceiling above your head.
- Your fingertips need to face inward.
- While you do this, push your other arm downward and leave your hands by your side.

Switch between your hands.

Twisting your spine

Follow the steps given below to perform this exercise:

- Place your hands in front of you. You need to pretend you are carrying an exercise ball.
- Leave your left leg above your head.
- Bend your knees slightly and turn your waist toward your left.

- The next thing to do is to switch between your hands. Lift the right hand and turn towards the right.
- Your back should be supple and upright.

Hips

Stretching forward

Follow the steps given below to stretch your hip forward:

- Move your left heel in front of your body and slowly push your hands back to maintain balance.
- Now, push your left leg back and rest your body on your toes.
- Stretch your hands forward and lift them to the height of your shoulders.
- Repeat the exercise on the other side.

An alternative to performing this exercise is to step on the toes of your other foot before moving the leg back.

Stretching sideways

- Push your hands to the side and visualize that you are pushing your body against a wall.
- Stretch your opposite foot to the side and stretch.

Knees

Kick

Follow the steps given below to perform this exercise:

- Loosen your fists and set your palms to your side.
- Leave your arms at the sides of your hips.
- Stretch one foot outward and pretend to make a kicking motion.
- While you do this, slowly punch your opposite fist outward. Your palms should face downward.

- Now move your arms and legs back. Repeat this process on the other side.

Stepping forward

- Place your fists close to your hips. Keep your knees relaxed.
- Now, step forward slightly with one foot.
- You can shift your weight onto the front foot.
- As your body moves forward, you need to punch using the opposite arm. You can do the same with the opposite side of the leg.

Ankles

Tapping the ankle

- You need to tap your feet using both your toes and heels.
- Alternate between your legs.

Ankle rotation

With your toes facing downward, lift your heel and move your foot in a clockwise direction thrice. Now, switch to the opposite direction. You can switch between your feet as well.

Chapter Nine: The 24-Move Sequence

This chapter will look at a 24-form sequence you need to follow when you perform Tai Chi regularly. The sequence of these movements is:

1. Commencing Form
2. Parting the Horse's Mane
3. White Crane Spreads its Wings
4. Brush Knee
5. Playing the Lute
6. Repulsing the Monkey
7. Grasping the Bird's Tail on the Right
8. Grasping the Bird's Tail on the Left
9. Single Whip
10. Cloud Hands
11. Single Whip
12. High Pat on the Horse
13. Kick Out with the Right Heel

14. Double Punch

15. Turn, Kick Out with the Left Heel

16. Serpent in the Grass on the Right, Golden Cockerel Stands on its Left Leg

17. Serpent in the Grass on the Left, Golden Cockerel Stands on its Right Leg

18. Maiden Working the Shuttles

19. Needle at the Bottom of the Sea

20. Flash Arms like a Fan

21. Turn, Deflect, Parry and Punch

22. Apparent Closing and Push

23. Cross Hands

24. Closing Form

You will now look at how you can perform each of these sequences in the next few sections.

Commencing Form

In this step, you work on your breathing and perform the following Qigong exercises.

Arm Raises

- Place your feet firmly on the ground and shoulder-width apart.
- Spread your weight evenly between your feet.
- Leave your arms to relax at your sides. Do not clench your fists.
- Take a deep breath in and raise your arms to shoulder level. You can move them higher if you feel comfortable.
- Keep your elbows soft and relaxed.
- Now, exhale slowly and lower your arms.

Opening Your Chest

- Stand with your feet firmly placed on the ground while ensuring your weight is spread evenly between your legs.
- Your arms should remain relaxed on either side.
- Take a deep breath and raise your arms to your shoulder level.
- While you exhale, you need to move your arms toward your center while ensuring your palms face each other.
- Move your arms to the middle of your chest. Bear in mind that your shoulders need to be relaxed.
- Now, lower your arms slowly.

Repeat this exercise until you feel relaxed.

Stretching Sideways

- Take a deep breath in and slowly lift your arms above your head. Your elbows should be relaxed and slightly bent. You need to shift your weight on either side.
- Now, lift your opposite arm in front of you and keep it straight. Maintain the position an archer does when they are firing a bow.
- Take another deep breath in and raise both your arms above your head. Now move the weight to the center of your body.
- Breathe out slowly and shift your weight from the right side of your body to the left.
- Mirror this form on the other side.

Repeat this exercise until you feel relaxed.

Bending and Circling Arms

- Stand comfortably on the ground. Maintain a firm form and keep your feet shoulder-width apart. You need to spread your weight evenly.

- Let your arms remain relaxed and loose by your sides.

- Now, cross your hands in front of your body with your palms facing toward you.

- Breathe in deeply and lift your arms above your head as high as you can.

- Now, breathe out and lower your arms slightly. Your elbows should be bent slightly while you return to the center position.

Twisting and swinging your arms

- Turn your body to the right. You should only twist at your waist. You can bend your knees slightly if you need to.

- Take a deep breath in and bend to your right. Move your right arm down the side of your body.

- Your palms should face upward while you move your arm backward in the shape of an arc.

- Lift your elbow to the height of your shoulders.

- Breathe out deeply and rotate your wrists until your palms move forward.

- Now, bring your right arm forward and shift your body weight forward until your arm is in front of you. Move your arms the way you would when you swim.

- Repeat the exercise on the other side.

If you have been practicing Tai Chi for a while, you will know how to perform this movement using both arms. If you are a beginner, you can work with one side at a time to move in the right manner.

Side Arm Rotations

- Take a deep breath in and lift your arms like you are cradling a child or baby.

- Your palms should face you while you turn to the left.

- Now twist your body at the waist to your right and move your weight onto your left foot. Focus on your left arm when you perform this movement.
- Your right hand should always be placed beneath the left arm. Exhale deeply and move back to the center.
- Take another deep breath and move toward your right.

When you perform this movement, the lower arm should always be close to your belly button while the upper arm is away from the middle.

Parting the Horse's Mane

You need to perform this movement three times when you perform Tai Chi. Your weight should be distributed equally between your legs. If you are unsure about how you should maintain your weight equally, follow the steps given below:

- Shift the weight to your left leg by slowly moving off your right leg.
- Lift your heel off the ground until there is no weight placed on your left leg.
- Now, place your leg back on the ground by lowering your toes first.
- Your weight should be distributed evenly between your legs.

To perform this movement, follow the steps given below:

- Stand firmly on the ground and wrap your arms around your thighs. It is best to wrap them around the middle but wrap your arms wherever comfortable if you cannot bend that much.
- Now, use your back muscles to lift your arms. Take a deep breath and move your arms to the chest level.
- Slowly bend downward and exhale deeply. Now, drop your elbows and shoulders using your core and back muscles.

- Now, place your right and left palms close to your belly button like you are holding a ball. The left arm should be placed on the bottom of the ball.

- Shift your legs so that they take the position of the letter T. Place your left foot on your toes to ensure there is no weight on the leg. Move your weight onto the right foot.

- Your right hand should be at your chest while your left hand is close to your belly button. Now, curve your fingers like you are holding the ball.

- Place your left foot now on its heel and maintain a 90-degree angle.

- Your left hand should move along with the left leg.

- Keep your knees open and flared.

- Your head should always be erect, and the weight should move to the center of your body.

- You need to move your left hand at the same time you move your hips. This will help you shift your weight evenly between your legs to maintain your posture.

- Now, stretch the knee of your right leg to ensure you do not flex or strain your back.

- Sit down until your left leg is on the heel and the weight shifts to the back foot. Now, flex your right knee, so your buttocks, back, and head are maintained in the same line.

- Next, pivot your heel until your leg is at a 45-degree angle. You need to align your hip and shift your weight onto the left foot. Now, align your hips.

- Step out of the position at a 90-degree angle and move the left hand toward the leg. Your fingers should be aligned together and away from the thumb.

- Move your hand toward the front of your body and open the palm slowly like you are serving your horse a meal.

- Move your right hand to your side and bend the elbow. The finger should be curved or rounded like you are holding the top of a ball. Your legs and hands should move simultaneously when you perform the movement.

- Now, sit down until your front foot is on the heel, but the weight is only on the back foot. Flex your knee to ensure your buttocks and back are maintained in a straight line.

White Crane Spreads Its Wings

To perform this exercise, follow the steps given below:

- Move your right step slightly forward. Do not place any weight on the right leg.

- Pretend you are holding onto a ball, but do not place any weight on your toes. Place your right hand at the bottom of the ball and your left hand on top.

- Now rotate or spin the ball while slowly shifting your weight from the front leg to the back leg. The ball should move in a counterclockwise direction.

- Lift your right hand upward and move it above your head. Your little finger should be in a position that allows you to cut the edge of the shoulder. Now, leave your hand in a relaxed form.

- Move the left hand to your side and maintain it in a cocked position. You need to bend the elbow and ensure your fingers are curved like they are placed on the top of the ball.

- Slowly shift your weight to the foot placed in the back. At the same time, you need to perform the following movements:

    - Sit down on your right foot.
    - Bend your left hand slightly at the elbow.
    - Place your left hand with the little finger pointing outward.

Brush Knee

To perform this stance, you need to follow the steps given below. You will perform this stance first using the left leg.

- Stand with your feet shoulder-distance apart and maintain a firm grip on the ground.
- Move your left foot until it faces the wall in front of you. The right foot should be pointed diagonally.
- Now, bend both your knees slightly and shift your weight to the front. Do not shift the full weight, but only 70 percent of your weight.
- Press your right hand forward and let your palm face the front wall. Leave your left hand on the thigh and relax.
- Now move your weight onto the right leg, which is at the back, and sit down on the leg. Shift your weight onto this leg.
- Your hands should remain in the same position but slowly expand. Do not turn your body at your waist.
- Now, turn your body at the waist toward your left. Let the left leg relax and turn outward to the left on your toes while your waist turns. Your palms should face you. Do not let your weight shift.
- Move your hips forward and shift the weight as well. Slowly move your hips diagonally and move the knee in. Push your right foot to the front and move your hips into a diagonal position.
- Shift the weight onto the left leg and maintain it until your right foot is off the floor. Then, move the right knee forward to meet the left knee.
- The right hand should now be at the center of your chest. Hold your arms like you are holding a ball.
- The left arm should move in line with your body. Leave the palms facing downward and at shoulder height. Do not turn your waist, but shift your weight diagonally.

- Now move your right leg, which does not have any weight on it, to the right side of your body. Do not move your weight in this step.

- Lower your right arm slowly and straighten the left arm until your palm faces upward. Now, bend your left elbow slowly and point your fingers to your ears.

- Turn your waist slightly toward the front wall but make sure not to shift your weight.

- Move your waist forward and shift your weight onto your right leg back to the initial weight shift.

- Lower your right hand until your hand is close to your leg. Let your hand rest against your thigh.

- Now, move the left arm until it is in front of you and turn the waist slowly while your palm faces the front of the shoulder.

You need to perform this exercise thrice.

Playing the Lute

Follow the steps given below to perform this exercise:

- When you perform this movement, you need to step forward. You need to move the right foot in front of you without placing too much weight on the leg. Move your right foot until you stand on your toes.

- Move the left hand above your head and keep it slightly bent.

- Now, move the right hand until your fingers are aligned to the left elbow. Bend the right hand slightly at the elbow and turn it inward. Do not maintain it parallel to the left hand.

- Move your weight slowly to the back leg. Your left leg may be a little wobbly when you start. You need to lift the heel off the ground and sit down carefully on your leg.

- Set the left heel firmly on the ground.
- Your hands need to be set in the right position, where your right hand is in line with the left elbow and is maintained in an inward position.
- Firmly place your heels on the ground while you shift your weight onto your left leg. Crouch by dropping your shoulders.
- Always maintain your balance and posture.

Repulsing the Monkey

Once you have performed the previous movement three times, move onto this movement. To perform this movement, follow the steps given below:

- Stand with your feet shoulder-width apart and place your heels firmly on the ground. Your weight should be distributed evenly between the legs.
- Move your left hand to the center of your body and shift your right hand to the back. Try to maintain a 90-degree angle using your right hand.
- Turn your neck and face toward the right hand as you move it.
- Keep your palms open and ensure they face upward at the same time.
- Now, look at your right hand and keep it higher than the left hand. Now turn your head and neck to follow the back hand as you move it.
- Lift your right hand higher than your left hand.
- While you do this, you need to move your weight onto your back leg. To do this, you need to move your front leg and lift it slightly.

- Now, stretch or extend your knee as you bring the leg back. You need to position the toe out and back so the leg is not on the same line as the front foot.

- Lower the toes until they are away from the front foot and turn the heel inward. Try to maintain a 45-degree angle.

- Move the back hand closer to the ear and follow the movement of the hand using your head.

- While you do this, you need to move the right foot forward to meet the center. Move your hands to the center while you push and pull them away from each other.

- The hand moving forward should always be at the center of the body. Your fingers should be curved, and your palms must face outward.

- Let your left hand move back while you curve the palm.

- Open the left hand and move it to your hip.

- Now, stretch the knee of your front leg and lower your body onto the back leg. Shift your weight slowly and carefully onto your leg to prevent any injury.

- Face the front when you perform this movement.

Repeat this movement on the other side. Before you do this, shift the weight to the center.

Grasping the Bird's Tail on the Right and Left

To perform this movement, follow the steps given below. Bear in mind that the steps to perform this movement on both the right and left sides are the same. You will look at how you can perform this movement on your left.

- You need to pivot your right foot using your heel.

- Now move your left foot away from the right foot, which will remain at the back.

- Hold the ball with your left hand on top and right hand at the bottom. You can shift the bottom hand toward your body to ensure your palms face you.

- Rotate your body and flip your hands. The hand at the bottom should face the upper hand.

- Lower both hands at the same time and make sure they are equidistant.

- Move your head backward and look at your hands as you move them toward the back. Now, rotate your body and square your waist and hips while you move your hands forward.

- When your right hand and left wrist meet, you can push your arms out and separate them.

- Sit back on your left leg slowly and shift your body weight onto the back leg. Now push your body forward and lower your left hand. Use your left heel to pivot your leg.

- Move back to the center and hold the ball as you maintain a T-step.

Single Whip

You have looked at how you can perform the movement in the previous chapter. You need to complete this movement at least three times on either side after performing the bird's tail.

Cloud Hands

To perform this movement, follow the steps given below:

- Stand with your feet facing the front and placed shoulder-width apart. Visualize that your head is being lifted from your crown

- Tuck your chin toward your chest and look forward. Relax your body and let your arms hang loose at your sides.
- Part your fingers gently and curve them slightly.
- Your palms should not face away from your body.
- Your tailbone should be tucked inward and your knees bent slightly.
- Now, breathe in slowly and turn your left arm to face your body. Hold your palm in line with the center of your chest and facing inward.
- Your left elbow should be maintained at the same level or below your left hand. Curve the fingers slightly inward.
- When you do this, you need to extend your right arm and maintain it at the height of your waist.
- Turn your right palm downward and curve your fingers slightly. Keep your elbows bent.
- Shift your weight slowly to the left leg while you turn your waist slowly. Your arms should follow your waist as you turn.
- Now, turn your right palm to face your body while you curve the fingers. Your left palm should face downward and the fingers need to point forward. You can curve them if you want to.
- Raise your right arm until it is at your shoulder's level and slowly lower your left hand until it is at your waist.
- Exhale and turn your body back to the center while you transfer the weight.
- Breathe in deeply and transfer the weight onto your right leg while turning your body to the right. Turn your arms along with your waist.
- Now, turn the left palm inward to face the body while you curve your fingers.

- The right palm should face downward with your fingers curved slightly. Lift the left arm to the height of your shoulders and drop the right hand to your waist.

- Now, breathe out slowly and twist your body back to the center. Shift your weight to the center when you do this.

- Take another deep breath in and perform the exercise eight times.

Once you finish the repetitions, you can move back to the starting position. Breathe out and let your arms relax at your sides.

High Pat on the Horse

You have looked at how you can perform the movement in the previous chapter. You can take a break before you perform this exercise if you are tired. You need to remember that your body is not used to this type of workout, and you may tire easily.

Kick Out with the Right and Left Heel

The following are some types of kicks you can perform with your heels.

Reverse Kick

When you perform this kick, you need to move backward while keeping the leg you want to kick with close to the standing leg. Since you are looking at kicking using the right heel, you need to move the right leg close to the left leg. Use your heel to strike the opponent. You need to deliver the kick by stepping backward. This type of kick is damaging since it uses a lot of power.

Type One

- Breathe in deeply and keep your feet shoulder-width apart. Relax your arms on either side of your body.

• Turn your body to the left and throw your right leg backward.

• Now, shift your weight onto your left leg and lift your right heel to hit the groin.

Type Two

• Breathe in deeply and keep your feet shoulder-width apart. Relax your arms on either side of your body.

• Turn your body to the left and throw your right leg backward.

• Now, shift your weight onto your left leg and lift your right heel to hit the shin.

Side Kick

The side kick is another movement you can perform. You need to shift your weight and move your body sideways. When you perform this movement, you can use two areas as the points of impact. You can use the heel or the outer edge of your foot to perform this movement. This movement is often used as an offensive movement in Tai Chi since it can damage your opponent.

Type One

• Breathe in deeply and keep your feet shoulder-width apart. Relax your arms on either side of your body.

• Lift your hands to block your chest.

• Now, shift your body weight to the left and slowly raise the right leg to the side and kick at the person's shin or heel.

Type Two

• Breathe in deeply and keep your feet shoulder-width apart. Relax your arms on either side of your body.

• Lift your hands to block your chest.

- Now, shift your body's weight to the left and slowly raise the right leg to the side and kick at the person's knee.

You need to perform this movement using your right heel before you move onto the double punch movement. Then move onto performing the exercise using your left heel.

Double Punch

To perform this movement, follow the steps given below:

- Stand with your feet shoulder-width apart and move your right leg in front of the left.
- Now, shift your weight gently from the back foot to the front.
- Create a fist using both hands and push both arms out in front of you. Push your right arm in front before your left arm.
- Now, shift your weight onto the back leg and pivot your feet around.

The Serpent in the Grass on the Right, Golden Cockerel Stands on Its Left Leg

When you finish kicking out with your left heel, you can perform this movement. Follow the steps given below to do this:

- You need to bring your serpent in. Stand with your feet firmly on the ground and hook your right hand. Shift this hand above the left hand and look at it.
- Move your right leg to the front and slowly shift your weight onto the back leg.
- Now, lower your body halfway and slowly shift your weight.
- Shift your body slightly and pivot using both feet. You can perform the serpent movement on the other side.

Perform this movement at least thrice on both sides.

The remaining movements, listed below, are easy to perform. The names clearly define how you need to perform these movements. It is important to remember how to balance your body and weight when you perform the following.

Maiden Working the Shuttles

To perform this movement, follow the steps mentioned below:

- Place your feet shoulder-width apart and relax your arms at your sides.
- Now, shift your right heel out and extend the knee.
- Move your hand to the right and shift your waist and hips.
- Shift your foot outward and then move your hand.
- Move your hand forward and back above your forehead while you breathe in and out (this is like moving a shuttlecock above your head).
- Lower your hand below and rotate your waist and hips.
- Now lower your body slowly onto the back leg and shift your weight onto the leg.
- Hold your hands in front of you as if you are holding a ball and push your legs in.
- Perform the same exercise with your other leg.

Repeat this movement three times before you move onto the next movement.

Needle at the Bottom of the Sea

To perform this step, follow the steps given below:

- Stand with your feet shoulder-width apart and move your arms back.
- Now, slowly lift your left leg. Lift it high enough so that your big toe touches the ground.

- Bend your right knee slightly and maintain the position.
- Lift your right hand and move it toward the left knee.
- Bend down slowly and reach toward the left big toe to find the needle.
- Slowly move your hand back up and straighten your back.
- Now, lower your foot and relax.

Repeat this exercise with your right leg.

Flash Arms Like a Fan

Once you repeat the previous movement three times on either side, you can relax before starting this movement.

- Stand with your feet shoulder-width apart. Let your hands relax on your thighs.
- Now, bend your right knee slightly and shift your weight onto the right leg.
- Lift your arms and keep the elbows bent.
- Stretch the back knee out as far as you can and lower yourself on your right leg.
- Come out of the position by releasing your arms and slowly moving your weight back to your center.
- Repeat this exercise with your left leg.

Turn, Deflect, Parry, and Punch

After performing the previous movement, you should come back to your center of balance before performing this movement.

- Stand with your feet shoulder-width apart and relax your arms at your sides. Slowly lift your arms upward and maintain them in front of you. Ensure the palms face away from you.

- Now, place your left foot forward and bend the knees slightly. Lift your left arm and maintain it parallel to your thigh. Lift your right arm and keep it underneath your left arm.

- Slowly shift your weight from the right leg onto the left by moving your back forward.

- Turn left using your hips and waist.

- Lift your right leg and move through the left leg. Now, your right leg is in front of you. Land on your heel. You need to move your arms the same way you did in step two, but with opposite hands.

- Turn to your right and move your left leg in front of your right leg. Now, slowly move back to the center.

When you perform this movement, you need to shift your weight slowly onto the leg you are placing in front of you. This is the only way you can maintain your balance throughout the movement.

The last two movements are the apparent closing and pushing. These movements are of utmost importance since you will use all the energy in your body. The pushing movement and how it works are explained in the next chapter.

Once you perform these movements, you can close off the form and stretch. Center your weight and balance yourself in the right position.

Chapter Ten: Pushing Hands: Eight Gates and Five Steps

Push hands is an important practice performed when you practice Tai Chi. When you perform this movement, you need to use the four directions, and it is best to perform this movement with someone else. If you use local strength or muscle, you cannot train using the energies in the four directions. When you perform this movement, you always need to maintain the energy. You also need to manifest the energy from different directions whenever your partner touches you. It is important to keep yourself relaxed when you do this.

The energy in your arms and hands is manipulated by the movements you make. You can easily work with this energy and manipulate it when you move your waist. To do this, you need to relinquish the control you exert from your shoulders and arms and relax your shoulders. It is only when you do this that the movement will have the necessary effects.

It is hard for you to control your arms using your waist since this is not something you are used to. You also need to let your waist control the way you move. You can start with the pushing hand movement using a single hand. You will move on to using both hands to perform this exercise in the next few steps. You need to practice the pattern carefully and fix the way you move before moving your arms freely. Practice this movement carefully.

Assume you are in combat. You may find yourself in a position where you are going to lose. It is during this time that you need to step out and let your partner win. Do not resist the win because that only leads to tension in the muscles. You may begin to use your local muscles to do this, which you need to stop. Do not develop any bad habits that could lead you away from using the energy in your body. Invest and learn from your losses.

When you are in combat, you need to ensure your opponent does not come too close to you. If you can control your opponent's direction and center, you can let them approach you. Most people lose in combat Tai Chi because they let their opponent enter their space without maintaining any control. When you perform Tai Chi, whether in combat or practice, you need to maintain some connection with the energy—this is the only way you can match your opponent.

Whenever you connect with your opponent, you need to ensure the contact is light. You should never try to hurt your opponent unless you are defending yourself. When you are in combat, learn to focus on your opponent's balance. Never let your arms and hands move too far away. They need to be close to your center. Never focus on your local muscles but consider your entire body.

Use your leg strength during combat. This is a way to overpower your opponent. If your legs are strong, you can source your power and energy from your lower body. When your source of energy is lower and stronger, you can push your hands easily and effectively. You need to monitor how you feel and how pure your energy is. You also need to check if you are relaxed or not and identify the areas that may have forced you to use too much strength. Learn to correct these movements to avoid any mistakes in the future. As mentioned earlier, you need to use the energy from your legs when you perform Tai Chi. You will soon learn to move away from people easily.

Eight Gates and Five Steps

When you perform Tai Chi, you need to control, cultivate, and unify your body's energy with the energy of the universe. This vital and primary energy in your body is termed qi. When you move, the muscles in your body use a form of energy termed li. This energy is bioelectric and is a purely physical form of energy. When you learn to combine the universal, primal energy with the physical energy, you develop energy in your body called jing or jen. This is the energy that powers every move you make is Tai Chi. The postures discussed in the previous chapter are powered by this energy only.

Most of the postures require much footwork. It is only when you manage to maintain your footwork that you can move your body smoothly from one posture to another. You can also maintain balance only when you manage your footwork. There are five steps used in each of these postures, and these are termed as the five steps. These patterns include the following steps:

- Maintaining central equilibrium
- Stepping forward
- Stepping backward
- Turning right
- Turning left

The other postures you maintain will help you determine how you express or use jing when you fight. These postures are termed as the eight gates or eight energies. You can connect these energies to the Tai Chi compass. You can divide these eight energies into four directions or four primary energies and four corners or four secondary energies. The primary energies are known as:

- Roll back
- Push
- Press forward

- Ward off

The secondary energies are known as:

- Shoulder stroke
- Elbow stroke
- Split
- Pull down

Every movement you make in Tai Chi is based on these blocks. You need to learn how to move continuously and smoothly between each of these blocks. When you master these blocks, you can combine, split, and recombine the movements until you find a sequence that works for you.

Chapter Eleven: Combat Tactics and Sequences

An important aspect to bear in mind is that Tai Chi is a martial art. You need to understand different fighting strategies to ensure you are not on the losing team. Wait for your enemy to attack your first, so you get to make the first contact. The following are some points to bear in mind.

Focus on Timing, Movement, and Distance

If you want to ensure your opponent attacks first, you need to maintain the right distance between yourself and the opponent. You also need to time your movements. It is also important for you to learn more about Tai Chi before choosing to fight with anybody else. Tai Chi refers to the use of energy and minimizing the number of movements you make.

Understanding the Physical Strategy

From what you have read, you should understand that Tai Chi is a moving martial art. It is important for you to learn how to use space and distance easily. You can use kicks or punches to determine the distance between yourself and your opponent. Understanding this is the essence or foundation of the strategy of Tai Chi. You should walk out of your attacker's range or enter it only when you know you can change the outcome to your advantage. Consider the following scenario to help you understand the same:

- Your enemy is around ten feet from you.
- You know they need to cover this distance if they want to attack you.
- This gives you enough time to plan your counterattack when your attacker moves toward you.
- You can hit your opponent before they reach you, as well.

Land the First Hit

Another way to look at the above scenario is that you invite your opponent to move into your attack zone so that you can evade their strikes. You only need to wait patiently to do this. When they enter your attack zone, you can strike them easily at their weakest point. If you are unsure of their weak point, you can pick your best movement and strike the attacker with the required speed. If your attacker moved carefully and struck you first, it is important to bear in mind that you took the last hit.

End the Fight with Little Force

The objective of every Tai Chi fight should be to end it without confronting the attacker with too much force. You only need to prevent the attacker from finding anywhere to strike.

Move Carefully

Consider how you would hang a shower curtain or towel. When you strike a shower curtain or towel very hard and fast, it will only bend or move. Do you think you can put a hole in this curtain or towel? If you have watched the karate kid movie starring Jackie Chan and Jaden Smith, you know this is quite possible. You cannot expect the towel or curtain to give away unless you make the required effort.

You need to look at how energy flows when you make any movement compared to how the curtain or towel moves. This will give you an idea of how you want your movements to flow and transition. Do you think you can be soft to ensure nobody can hit you and cause harm? You can do this, but you will need to practice to know how you can move in this way.

Become Hard

When you want to attack your opponent, you need to become a solid object. This is the only way you can use your body weight to transmit all your energy to attack your opponent.

Throw in Some Yin and Yang

If you move from a flowing and soft motion like a shower curtain or towel to a connected and solid piece, you will learn to display the concept of yin and yang when you fight. Relax before you start the fight and wait until you want to strike your opponent. When your opponent is close to you, see how you can transfer the weight in one strike.

Chapter Twelve: Daily Tai Chi Practice

The movements of Tai Chi are gentle, flowing, and smooth. Through these movements, you learn to treat your body to a relaxing and gentle workout. You can say goodbye to workouts that make you pant, puff, and sweat. You will feel energized, refreshed, cool and calm after a Tai Chi workout. Spend only fifteen minutes every day if you want to improve your fitness, health, and peace of mind. You have looked at the benefits of Tai Chi earlier in the book, and you can reap these benefits if you perform Tai Chi for at least ten minutes every day. You will see that your body and mind work in harmony.

You can try the different Tai Chi exercises and Qigong exercises mentioned in this book. They are fun, and you should enjoy performing them, too. You can perform a relaxing Tai Chi exercise if you are stressed or having a terrible day at work. The following are some tips you need to bear in mind if you want to integrate Tai Chi into your workout and daily routine.

Tips

Be Open

The first thing to bear in mind is to keep yourself open to the energy of the universe. You need to learn to develop this connection between everything in your surrounding environment. Learn to relax.

Observe Nature

When you perform Tai Chi exercises, you focus on your breathing and the surrounding environment. You need to observe everything happening in nature around you. Focus on the wind, rain, sun, and stillness. Notice how the energy is flowing from one entity to the next around you.

Be Aware of Your Connection

You should become aware of where you are seated. Find your connection with the ground and develop on that connection. According to Huang Sheng-Shyan, "*If you practice (a martial art) without paying attention to your gong (base), then it will be a lifetime of empty practice.*"

Find the Connection to Your Whole Body

You need to learn how to let the energy from within you flow through your consciousness. Let the movement of this energy rise from the source within you. According to Wee Kee-Jin, "*Moving the arms is not Tai Chi – your arms do move, but they move dependent upon initiation of movement from the base, not on their own.*"

Be Consistent

As with any other exercise regime or workout, you need to be consistent if you want to make steady progress.

Practice with People

If you know you cannot do it alone, you can work with someone who supports you and your aspirations. Speak to a friend or your family and see if anybody is willing to perform Tai Chi with you.

Choose a friend or family member who will support you and help you maintain discipline. If you are conscious about doing it alone, take someone with you.

Either Workout Barefoot or Wear Thin Shoes

You need to find a way to connect to the earth. To do this, you can either wear thin-soled shoes or perform Tai Chi barefoot. You can buy Tai Chi shoes if you need to, which allow you to connect easily to the earth and make it easier for the earth's energy to move throughout your body. You can wear softer shoes regularly to continue to feel the energy from the earth.

Learn to Forgive

When you perform Tai Chi, you try to rid your body of any toxic energy. You need to let your heart and mind let go of the past and toxic memories. This enables you to focus on the present and accept the future with an open mind. Forgive yourself and people for any bad memories from the past.

Focus on Your Movements

You need to shift your energy and weight when you perform any Tai Chi movement. You have looked at this in detail in the book. Pay attention to your every movement throughout the day. This helps you determine how the energy flows in your body.

Identify the Yin and Yang in You

As a Tai Chi practitioner, you need to find the Yin and Yang energies within you. Each of these energies contains the other. Find the balance between these energies and in your life. Accept yourself for who you are.

Chapter Thirteen: What to Expect from Your First Class

If you choose to take a Tai Chi class to master the movements and footwork, you need to keep some points in mind. It is important to remember that Tai Chi classes will vary because of the location, instructor, and the Tai Chi style you are practicing. Now, look at some things you can expect from the class.

Meditative and Quiet Surroundings

When you work out with a large group of people, you tend to work in a gym or at a fitness center. The place is always noisy and bustling since people enter and leave after their workout. These places have upbeat music playing. Tai Chi is a very different art form, and it is meditative in nature. You need to find yourself in a quiet and calm environment if you want to practice Tai Chi. Most instructors choose to hold Tai Chi classes outdoors, but this is not always possible. If classes are held indoors, there is no loud music to interrupt your thoughts. The environment is soft and quiet. Every participant is also expected to respect the environment and maintain calm.

A Diverse Group

Anyone can perform Tai Chi. This means there is no age restriction. When you enter a class, you may find people from all walks of life around you, which should not surprise you. You need to embrace diversity because Tai Chi classes are different from regular fitness classes.

You can enroll yourself in a Tai Chi class if you are a beginner or an expert. If you are a beginner, you may feel overwhelmed when you find some members doing better than you. This should not worry you because you will improve over time. When you enter your class, choose a spot where you are comfortable and focus on the movements and energy flow. Focus on what the instructor has to say to you.

Nobody in class will look at you because each member is focusing only on their movements. You do not have to feel awkward. You may find people around you who will help you if you need to correct your movement.

Introduction to Tai Chi

Your instructor will tell you a little bit about Tai Chi before you start the class if you are a beginner. Most instructors do not give you much information about what Tai Chi is, but this book has everything you need to know. An instructor will expect you to have some idea about what Tai Chi is and will work on expanding that knowledge.

Warm-Up

It is important to warm your body up before you perform any exercise. You need to perform each warm-up exercise carefully since these exercises prepare your body for the movements you will make during the class. Tai Chi is a full-body workout, and it makes sense for you to prepare for the session. Most warm-up sessions use easy and gentle motions. Some exercises may include pacing, walking, rotating your shoulders, moving your head in either direction, clenching your hands, rocking on your toes, and more. It is during this time that you need to move into the right headspace. You need to clear your emotions and thoughts. Let go of any stress by preparing your mind to concentrate on the task at hand.

Breathing Exercises

You have looked at the importance of breathing when it comes to Tai Chi, and this is something every instructor will make you do at the start of the class. It is important to learn to breathe slowly and deeply when you perform Tai Chi. When you learn to breathe in this way, you relax both your mind and body. It also becomes easier to focus on your energy or qi. An instructor may choose one of the different meditation techniques discussed in the book.

Stretches

Before you begin to perform the different movements, you need to stretch your body's muscles to loosen them up, just like you do with most sports. An instructor can choose to perform easy to intense warm-up exercises depending on the movements being performed in class. You have looked at a few stretches you can perform at the start of the class for your knees, spine, hip, neck, and shoulders. You can repeat these stretches until you feel relaxed.

Instruction of Movements

This is the main part of your class since you learn the different forms and movements in Tai Chi. At the start of the class, the instructor will show you a few combinations or groups of movements. You may hear strange names being called out while depicting a certain movement. It is easier to use these names since they depict the exact movement you need to perform. There are different combinations and drills you can ask the instructor to teach you.

Repetition of Movements

When the instructor has taught students the movements and demonstrated each movement's flow, they will repeat it for you. They will also expect you to follow them as they repeat the movements. They may walk around the class and correct students who have trouble with performing some of the movements. If you are struggling with any form or movement, you can ask your instructor for further assistance. In Tai Chi, you must learn how to perform every movement correctly. It will take some time to master these movements and forms. If you are practicing Tai Chi for the first time, you may feel slightly disoriented after class. The trick is to stick with the practice so that you improve over time.

Relaxation and Cool Down

Regardless of the type of exercise you perform, you need to cool down and relax the muscles used during the workout. You need to spend some time breathing and stretching at the end of a Tai Chi class. Some instructors use this time to speak to you about applying different movements and techniques in your everyday life. At the end of the class, you will notice that you are more connected to your environment than before. While you cool down, try to focus on the different areas in your life where you can use the movements you performed in class. After you have cooled down, spend some time talking with the people around you.

Socialize

Many people join a club or class because they want to meet new people. When you are in a Tai Chi class, you cannot chat with your neighbors in class. You can mingle with them after class for a short while if you have the time. It is best to learn more about your group during this time. You will also make a lot of friends. Since you spend a few hours with these people every week, you will feel better when you learn more about them.

You can also speak to the instructor to learn more about them if you need to. You can talk to them about any issues or difficulties you may have with some of the movements. Since Tai Chi is a meditative martial art form, you need some time to adjust to your life after class. So, take this time after class to adjust and go back to your work.

Conclusion

If you are new to Tai Chi, you may not know that Tai Chi is a martial arts technique that originated in China. This art is an internal martial art, and it uses round, soft, and slow movements. Through Tai Chi, you will learn to redirect your energy and your opponent's energy through simple movements.

This book should have left you with information about what Tai Chi is and how it benefits you. It also shed some light on the different movements in Tai Chi and how you can master those movements. The book also gave you some Qigong exercises to perform before you begin the sequence of movements. If you follow the instructions in the book carefully, you can improve your overall health and wellbeing.

Since Tai Chi is a form of martial arts, you need to learn how to defend yourself. You also need to have some tricks up your sleeve to ensure you beat your opponent when you spar. This book has some tips and strategies you can use to help you to defeat your opponent.

Thank you for purchasing the book. Hopefully, you develop a habit to practice Tai Chi regularly to improve your mental, physical, spiritual, and emotional wellbeing.

Here's another book by Mari Silva that you might like

MARI SILVA
ORISHAS

THE ULTIMATE GUIDE TO AFRICAN ORISHA DEITIES AND THEIR PRESENCE IN YORUBA, SANTERIA, VOODOO, AND HOODOO, ALONG WITH AN EXPLANATION OF DILOGGUN DIVINATION

Your Free Gift (only available for a limited time)

Thanks for getting this book! If you want to learn more about various spirituality topics, then join Mari Silva's community and get a free guided meditation MP3 for awakening your third eye. This guided meditation mp3 is designed to open and strengthen ones third eye so you can experience a higher state of consciousness. Simply visit the link below the image to get started.

https://spiritualityspot.com/meditation

References

Byrne, K. (2017, June 1). A Brief History of Tai Chi in China. Culture Trip. https://theculturetrip.com/asia/china/articles/a-brief-history-of-tai-chi-in-china/

Caldwell, K. L., Bergman, S. M., Collier, S. R., Triplett, N. T., Quin, R., Bergquist, J., & Pieper, C. F. (2016). Effects of Tai Chi chuan on anxiety and sleep quality in young adults: lessons from a randomized controlled feasibility study. Nature and science of sleep, 8, 305–314. https://www.dovepress.com/effects-of-tai-chi-chuan-on-anxiety-and-sleep-quality-in-young-adults--peer-reviewed-fulltext-article-NSS

Chan, A. W., Yu, D. S., Choi, K. C., Lee, D. T., Sit, J. W., & Chan, H. Y. (2016). Tai Chi qigong as a means to improve night-time sleep quality among older adults with cognitive impairment: a pilot randomized controlled trial. Clinical interventions in aging, 11, 1277–1286. https://www.dovepress.com/tai-chi-qigong-as-a-means-to-improve-night-time-sleep-quality-among-ol-peer-reviewed-fulltext-article-CIA

Every day Tai Chi. (n.d.). Everydaytaichi.org. http://www.everydaytaichi.org/

Five Steps and Eight Energies - Tai Chi Transformation. (n.d.). Taichitransformation.com. http://taichitransformation.com/primal13_energy.php

Frantzis, B. (2010, September 16). Tai Chi Meditation. Energy Arts. https://www.energyarts.com/tai-chi-meditation/

FUNDAMENTAL FOOTWORK. (n.d.). Www.taichiaustralia.com. https://www.taichiaustralia.com/articles/Fundamental_Footwork.htm

Harvard Health Publishing. (2019, August 20). The health benefits of Tai Chi - Harvard Health. Harvard Health; Harvard Health. https://www.health.harvard.edu/staying-healthy/the-health-benefits-of-tai-chi

Heel Kick (Taijiquan Movement). (n.d.). Modern Wushu Wiki. https://modern-wushu.fandom.com/wiki/Heel_Kick_(Taijiquan_Movement)

Helmer, J. (n.d.). Tai Chi and Qi Gong: Better Balance and Other Benefits. WebMD. https://www.webmd.com/fitness-exercise/a-z/tai-chi-and-chi-gong

History of Tai Chi. (n.d.). Www.seas.ucla.edu. http://www.seas.ucla.edu/spapl/qifeng/history.html

How Tai Chi Breathing Can Make You Better, Faster, Stronger. (2017, March 29). Openfit. https://www.openfit.com/tai-chi-breathing-how-to-benefits

Hui, S. S.-C., Xie, Y. J., Woo, J., & Kwok, T. C.-Y. (2015, October 12). *Effects of Tai Chi and Walking Exercises on Weight Loss, Metabolic Syndrome Parameters, and Bone Mineral Density: A Cluster Randomized Controlled Trial*. Evidence-Based Complementary and Alternative Medicine. https://www.hindawi.com/journals/ecam/2015/976123/

Integrate Tai Chi into Your Daily Routine - Acufinder.com. (n.d.). Acufinder.com.

https://www.acufinder.com/Acupuncture+Information/Detail/Integrate+Tai+Chi+into+Your+Daily+Routine

Jerry. (2019, May 25). What is the Dantian? Balanced Life Tai Chi. https://balancedlifetaichi.com/blog/so02csj1tgsp74hlwwlk6en8ybjv19

Lam, P. (2014, January 28). History of Tai Chi. Tai Chi for Health Institute. https://taichiforhealthinstitute.org/history-of-tai-chi-2/

LaMeaux, E. C. (n.d.). 4 Tai Chi Meditation Techniques. Gaiam. https://www.gaiam.com/blogs/discover/4-tai-chi-meditation-techniques

Li, F., Harmer, P., Fitzgerald, K., Eckstrom, E., Stock, R., Galver, J., Maddalozzo, G., & Batya, S. S. (2012). Tai Chi and Postural Stability in Patients with Parkinson's Disease. New England Journal of Medicine, 366(6), 511–519. https://www.nejm.org/doi/full/10.1056/NEJMoa1107911

Mortazavi, H., Tabatabaeichehr, M., Golestani, A., Armat, M. R., & Yousefi, M. R. (2018). The Effect of Tai Chi Exercise on the Risk and Fear of Falling in Older Adults: a Randomized Clinical Trial. Materia socio-medica, 30(1), 38–42. https://www.ejmanager.com/mnstemps/16/16-1518555232.pdf?t=1623002592

Nordqvist, J. (2018, August 30). Tai Chi: Benefits, types, and history. Www.medicalnewstoday.com. https://www.medicalnewstoday.com/articles/265507

Sauer, M. (2018, May 14). Tai Chi Benefits: Stress Reduction, Weight Loss, for Older Adults. Healthline. https://www.healthline.com/health/tai-chi-benefits#arthritis

Shojai, P. (2019, January 6). What is Qi Gong? Your Guide to This Asian Yoga Practice. Yoga Journal. https://www.yogajournal.com/yoga-101/what-is-qi-gong/

Signam, M. (n.d.). Guidelines for Pushing Hands by Mike Sigman. Www.wooddragon.org.uk. http://www.wooddragon.org.uk/tai_chi_push_hands.html

Tai Chi: Definition and History - Tai Chi Association Colorado Springs, LLC. (2012, June 3). Tai Chi Association Colorado Springs, LLC. https://taichicoloradosprings.com/tai-chi-definition-and-history/

Tai Chi and Qi gong: What is the difference? (n.d.). Learn Tai Chi with the Teaptomonk: Courses. Articles, Videos, Books and More. https://www.teapotmonk.com/the-difference-between-taichi-and-qigong.html

Tai Chi Breathing: 9 Guidelines to Improve Practice. (2016, August 1). Tai Chi Basics. https://taichibasics.com/tai-chi-breathing/

Tai Chi Philosophy And Application in Daily Life. (n.d.). Golden Lion Academy. https://www.goldenlion.com.au/tai-chi/history-tai-chi/philosophy/

Taichi — Exercise for Daily Life - Dr. Greg Yuen. (n.d.). Gregyuenmd.com. https://gregyuenmd.com/taichi-exercise-for-daily-life/

The difference between Tai Chi and qi gong. (n.d.). Www.piedmont.org. https://www.piedmont.org/living-better/the-difference-between-tai-chi-and-qi-gong

The Tai Chi Walk - Walking Brush Knee and Press. (2010, June 9). Just Breathe — Tai Chi | Qigong | Yoga. https://zen.thisistruecs.com/2010/06/the-tai-chi-walk-walking-brush-knee-and-press/

The Three Dantians. (2013, July 1). Tai Chi Basics. https://taichibasics.com/three-dantians/

Top 10 Tips For Tai Chi Beginners | realbuzz.com. (n.d.). Realbuzz 5. https://www.realbuzz.com/articles-interests/fitness/article/top-10-tips-for-tai-chi-beginners/

Uhlig, T., Fongen, C., Steen, E., Christie, A., & Ødegård, S. (2010). Exploring Tai Chi in rheumatoid arthritis: a quantitative and qualitative study. BMC musculoskeletal disorders, 11, 43. https://doi.org/10.1186/1471-2474-11-43

Wang, C., Schmid, C. H., Fielding, R. A., Harvey, W. F., Reid, K. F., Price, L. L., Driban, J. B., Kalish, R., Rones, R., & McAlindon, T. (2018). Effect of Tai Chi versus aerobic exercise for fibromyalgia: comparative effectiveness randomized controlled trial. BMJ (Clinical research ed.), 360, k851. https://doi.org/10.1136/bmj.k851

Wang, C., Schmid, C. H., Hibberd, P. L., Kalish, R., Roubenoff, R., Rones, R., & McAlindon, T. (2009). Tai Chi is effective in treating knee osteoarthritis: a randomized controlled trial. Arthritis and rheumatism, 61(11), 1545–1553. https://onlinelibrary.wiley.com/doi/full/10.1002/art.24832

Warm Up and Stretching Exercises | Tai Chi for Health Institute. (2013, December 12). Tai Chi for Health Institute. https://taichiforhealthinstitute.org/warm-up-and-stretching-exercises/

What are the differences between Qigong and Tai Chi? (2017, May 8). Qigong Online by Space to Relax. https://spacetorelax.com/differences-qigong-tai-chi/

What is Tai Chi? | Tai Chi for Health Institute. (2018). Tai Chi for Health Institute. https://taichiforhealthinstitute.org/what-is-tai-chi/

Wu, W., Liu, X., Wang, L., Wang, Z., Hu, J., & Yan, J. (2014). Effects of Tai Chi on exercise capacity and health-related quality of life in patients with chronic obstructive pulmonary disease: a systematic review and meta-analysis. International journal of chronic obstructive pulmonary disease, 9, 1253–1263. https://www.dovepress.com/effects-of-tai-chi-on-exercise-capacity-and-health-related-quality-of--peer-reviewed-fulltext-article-COPD

Yeung, A., Chan, J. S. M., Cheung, J. C., & Zou, L. (2018). Qigong and Tai-Chi for Mood Regulation. FOCUS, 16(1), 40–47. https://focus.psychiatryonline.org/doi/10.1176/appi.focus.20170042

Zheng, S., Kim, C., Lal, S., Meier, P., Sibbritt, D., & Zaslawski, C. (2017). The Effects of Twelve Weeks of Tai Chi Practice on Anxiety in Stressed But Healthy People Compared to Exercise and Wait-List Groups-A Randomized Controlled Trial. Journal of Clinical

Psychology, 74(1), 83-92.
https://onlinelibrary.wiley.com/doi/abs/10.1002/jclp.22482

Printed in Great Britain
by Amazon